BUTCHERS,
BONNET MAKERS
&

A forgotten diary of daily life in early Victorian Cannock

June Pickerill

Published by
Mount Chase Press
109 Mount Street, Hednesford, Cannock, Staffs. WS12 4DB
01543 422891

ISBN 978-0-9551382-5-6

Designed and produced by John Griffiths, printed in the UK

CONTENTS

Acknowledgements (i)

List of Maps and Photographs (ii) – (iii)

Foreword (iv)

Cannock in the 1840's 1

Mary Lindop's Diary 1838 – 1846 19

1 Part of the Lindop Family Tree 147

2 Thomas Lindop's Wills 148

3 Index of People 149

Bibliography 156

ACKNOWLEDGEMENTS

Many thanks to the staff of the various local archive centres, including Cannock, Lichfield, Stafford and Wolverhampton, whose help and patience proved invaluable whilst researching the many aspects of the historical events of the diary.

Also thanks to David Battersby and Mr. N. Bailey who lent postcards and pictures of the local area and also the Cheslyn Hay Local Historical Society who helped with the information on the Shorter family and to Bev Hindley for the illustration of fashion.

Also thanks to Tony Hunt for his time-consuming research on the Cannock Parish Records and Tithe Maps as well as accompanying me to take photographs of the graveyard at Eccleshall.

I also would like to mention members of my own family, in particular my granddaughter Helena, for their assistance in computer skills which sadly your author lacks.

Please note that all photographs were used in good faith, but apologies to anyone whose copyright may have been unintentionally infringed.

LIST OF MAPS & PHOTOGRAPHS

MAPS

1.   Chatcull Tithe Map 1846.   2
2.   Residences of branches of the Lindop family.   3
3.   Calving Hill Tithe Map 1841.   4
4.   Longford Road Area Tithe Map 1841.   5
5.   Places visited in the Diary.   17
6.   Cannock Town Centre 1841 Tithe Map.   18

PHOTOGRAPHS

1.   Holy Trinity Church, Eccleshall.   1
2.   Lindop Family graves, Eccleshall Churchyard.   2
3.   The Crown Inn, Cannock, and butchers' shop.   6
4.   Chatcull.   10
5.   Women at water pump, Cannock.   16
6.   The Old Conduit House, Cannock.   17
7.   Market Square, Cannock.   22
8.   Mr. Poyner's sheep.   25
9.   Teddesley Hall, Penkridge.   27
10. Hedge cutting, late nineteenth century.   28
11. Hatherton Hall.   29
12. Market Place, Cannock.   31
13. Advert for Blare's Pills.   32
14. Grave of William Lindop, Eccleshall Churchyard.   34
15. Bandstand and Bowling Green, Cannock.   35
16. Bloxwich Church and High Street, Walsall.   35
17. Mill Street, Cannock.   37
18. Market Place, Cannock.   39
19. Bowling Green cottages, Hatherton.   41
20. Pinfold Farm, Watling Street, Norton.   45
21. Huntington.   46
22. Walsall Road, Cannock.   48
23. Advert for sale at Lord Hatherton's Estate.   49
24. Horse Fair, Rugeley.   50
25. Mr. Stubb's house on the left in Cannock.   51

26. Advert for the Sale at Pillaton Hall.   52
27. Pillaton Old Hall, Penkridge.   52
28. The Hall, Norton.   54
29. Pillaton Old Hall.   55
30. Sketch of St. Luke's Church with Poyner's house next door c. 1840.   60
31. Gathering hay c.1900.   60
32. Mowing grass c. 1900.   63
33. Chatcull old farm.   67
34. Lady from Longford House.   68
35. Advert of Bloxwich Races 1840.   70
36. Farm workers' lunchtime.   71
37. Harvest time c.1900.   73
38. Horses in field.   77
39. Norton Canes Parish Church.   78
40. Country walk around Longford c. 1900.   80
41. Four Crosses, Hatherton.   82
42. Walsall High Street.   83
43. Horse Fair, Rugeley.   87
44. Little Wyrley Hall.   91
45. Shops in Market Square, Cannock.   93
46. New Penkridge Road School.   96
47. Saredon.   98
48. Newspaper cutting of Mr. Pratt's race.   98
49. New Penkridge Road, Cannock.   101
50. Advert for sale at Mr. Miller's, Otherton.   102
51. The Hall, Norton Canes.   104
52. Cannock.   105
53. The Whitehouse's home and blacksmith's forge, Hatherton.   112
54. Preaching Cross, Cannock.   112
55. Wedges Mill.   114
56. Little Wyrley Hall.   116
57. The Cottage, Chatcull – home of the Barlow family.   118
58. Shoal Hill, Cannock.   124
59. The Crown Inn, Cannock, an old coaching inn.   129
60. Cannock Square.   132
61. A corner of old Cannock.   136
62. Cannock.   140
63. Trinity Church, Eccleshall.   142

FOREWORD

What was life really like in the middle of the 19th Century?

This Diary gives a unique and fascinating glimpse of the family life of ordinary folks at work and at play and encompasses most of the local population.

You may find one of your ancestors going about their daily work at the Mill, in the fields or as tradesmen, doctors, school teachers, servants, all busy coming together as a community; celebrating the twenty-first birthday of the son of Lord Hatherton and joyously joining in the Coronation of young Queen Victoria and her subsequent marriage to Prince Albert; marvelling at the first railway in the area, in time replacing the canal, stage coach and horse and cart as a means of travel.

Cannock was just on the edge of the Industrial Revolution and before extensive coal mining in the area.

Not in existance was running water in their houses (although Cannock was luckier than most), no gas or electricity, relying solely on oil lamps and candles, no lights in the streets, in the winter one fire for heating and cooking and very few good roads.

However, Cannock was a typical English country town.

CANNOCK IN THE 1840s

A chance meeting a number of years ago took me back in time to the middle of the 19th century, when a diary that had lain forgotten from that time surfaced and gave rare glimpses of daily life in Cannock of ordinary people , both the mundane and important events. Almost written in code, as a local historian, I could not resist the challenge of transcribing this diary in its authentic form for the purpose of making it available for everyone to enjoy.

I have transcribed it as it is written, bearing in mind that in 1840/41 most people were illiterate, therefore spelling is not as now, and sometimes can be misleading.

To understand the events mentioned in the diary, knowledge is needed about the entire family, down to grandparents, together with the residents of Cannock and surrounding areas, to see how they relate and interact with one another.

It is quite a complicated family, as were many others in the 19th century, due to early deaths, remarriage, and most of all, by all the generations handing down the same Christian names throughout the family, made no easier by the writer of the diary, who I believe was the 12 year old daughter of the family, using initials only when mentioning family members. Of course she would have known who they were and research has helped to put the appropriate names to these initials. A stroke of luck, when it was realised that the diary was written just as the 1841 Census was taken.

To determine who the different family groups were, a starting point was made with the Lindop family of the middle to late 18th century who originated from Wyenbury in the County of Cheshire , moving there it is believed, due to religious persecution.

Richard Lindop (1749-1805) married Frances Bettenson on 10.9.1781, producing ten children, namely William, Richard, Joseph, Mary, Ann, John, Thomas, Sarah, Eliza and James, all born between 1784 and the end of the century, and living at Old Hall Farm, Chatcull, near Eccleshall.

Frances the "Grandmother at Chatcull" lived to the great age of 91 years and is interred at Eccleshall. Her son John stayed at the farm with his wife Mary and four children, John, Abraham, Jane and Ann, helping Frances with the rearing of the

Holy Trinity Church, Eccleshall.

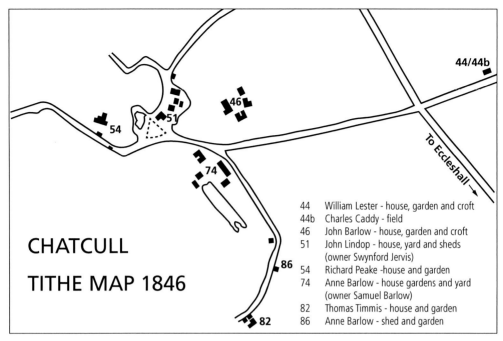

44   William Lester - house, garden and croft
44b   Charles Caddy - field
46   John Barlow - house, garden and croft
51   John Lindop - house, yard and sheds
        (owner Swynford Jervis)
54   Richard Peake -house and garden
74   Anne Barlow - house gardens and yard
        (owner Samuel Barlow)
82   Thomas Timmis - house and garden
86   Anne Barlow - shed and garden

CHATCULL

TITHE MAP 1846

cattle and making great quantities of cheese.

William, the eldest, son married Elizabeth Bettenson, producing no children – he then remarried to Martha, producing four children, namely James, William, Joseph and Ann, and farming at Milton. His death is recorded in the diary in 1840 at the age of 56 years.

The three family graves.

Second eldest son Richard married Mary and they produced John, Thomas, William, Mary Ann, James. Caroline and Eliza. Richard died in 1832 aged 46 years leaving his wife Mary to run the farm at Hatherton with the help of her children. She died in 1861 aged 74 years.

Third son Joseph married Elizabeth producing five children, William, Joseph, Amelia, Edmund and Clara. They farmed at Little Wyrley, Norton, Cannock, and in the 1851 Census had Elizabeth Lindop living with them, sister of Richard Lindop of Chatcull, and Joseph's aunt, aged 89 years.

The fourth son Thomas married twice, his first wife Mary nee Hand, having a daughter Sarah Eliza, Mary dying in 1821. His second wife, Mary nee Walker produced an additional five children, Thomas, Mary, Richard, George and William.

This family is the family of the Diary.

Thomas was a butcher and farmer, with the family living in a house and shop adjacent to the Crown Hotel in Cannock (later known as Dicky Wright's butchers shop). Wife Mary died in 1852 aged 47 years and Thomas died on 19.5.1857 aged 65 years. He owned land and property in and around Cannock, the income from this amounted to

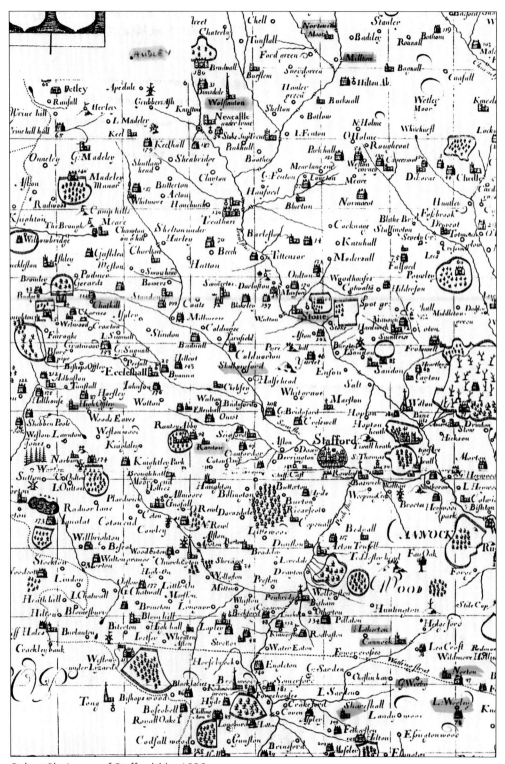

Robert Plot's map of Staffordshire 1686.
Lindop family residencies (Shaded). Other Lindops found plus village of Audley which is just above Newcastle-under-Lyme but not on the map.

£3.6.10d. He also rented additional land at Calving Hill and in the Longford Road area. Arable farming was the main occupation, growing such crops as Barley to make malt for whiskey, Oats, Wheat, Hay, Peas, Potatoes, Turnips, and also Clover. He was also a tenant of Lord Hatherton, travelling to Walsall to pay his rent.

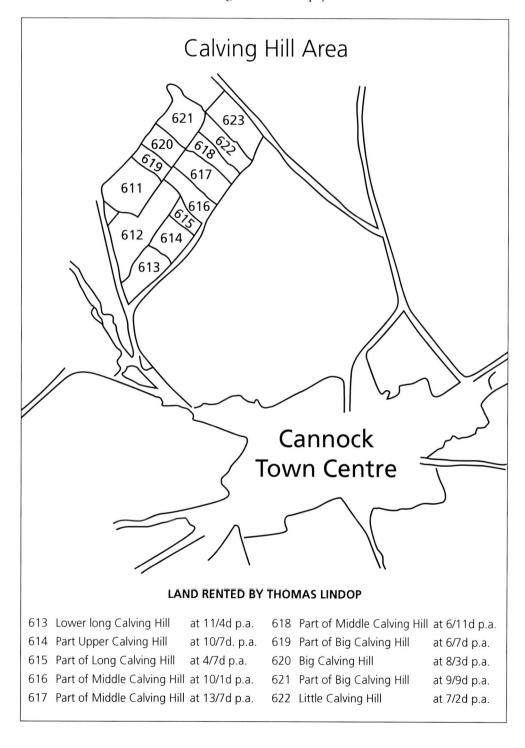

Calving Hill Area

Cannock Town Centre

LAND RENTED BY THOMAS LINDOP

613	Lower long Calving Hill	at 11/4d p.a.	618	Part of Middle Calving Hill	at 6/11d p.a.
614	Part Upper Calving Hill	at 10/7d. p.a.	619	Part of Big Calving Hill	at 6/7d p.a.
615	Part of Long Calving Hill	at 4/7d p.a.	620	Big Calving Hill	at 8/3d p.a.
616	Part of Middle Calving Hill	at 10/1d p.a.	621	Part of Big Calving Hill	at 9/9d p.a.
617	Part of Middle Calving Hill	at 13/7d p.a.	622	Little Calving Hill	at 7/2d p.a.

As a butcher, he bought cows, calves, pigs, sheep and lambs from as far away as Fazeley, Dunston, Teddesley, Pillaton, and Wolverhampton, Stafford and Rugeley Fairs. It is not clear if all his stock was butchered to sell in the shop, or whether he also butchered animals owned by various local people for their own use. Perhaps it was both. He also sold copious amounts of cheese, which he bought from his mother's farm at Chatcull.

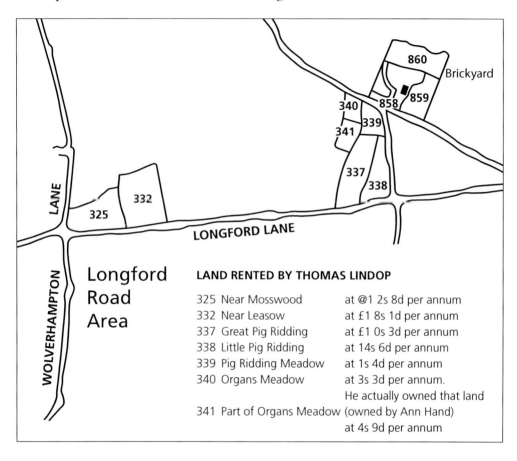

LAND RENTED BY THOMAS LINDOP

325	Near Mosswood	at @1 2s 8d per annum
332	Near Leasow	at £1 8s 1d per annum
337	Great Pig Ridding	at £1 0s 3d per annum
338	Little Pig Ridding	at 14s 6d per annum
339	Pig Ridding Meadow	at 1s 4d per annum
340	Organs Meadow	at 3s 3d per annum. He actually owned that land
341	Part of Organs Meadow	(owned by Ann Hand) at 4s 9d per annum

When animals and cheese were brought from Chatcull the meeting place was Stafford, which was roughly half way between Cannock and Chatcull. The animals would have been herded on foot and rested for a couple of days at Stafford before continuing their journey to Cannock.

The butcher's shop, next to the Crown Inn, in the middle of the town, was in a very good position, but there is no mention of shop staff. Was it open every day, except of course Sunday? And were the opening hours long? Thomas frequently travelled to all the local Fairs and so was obviously not behind the counter all the time. It is wondered whether perhaps the writer of the diary, daughter Mary, was the assistant, as plenty of gossip appears daily, seeming to be the centre for news of who had recently passed away, illnesses, births and marriages, and anything else likely to cause a stir among the residents such as the new Vicar, and where the previous one had taken up residence, hot air ballooning, the new fire engine, and above all, the advent of the railway, the cutting

The Crown Inn.

edge technology at that time. This enabled people to make use of the freedom of much faster travel and increasing the number of visitors to the town.

The properties that he owned in Mill Street he rented out to Betty Darby and her three adult children, Mary Askey and her three young children, William and Mary Lockley with their two babies and possibly Mr. Price who paid £1.0.0d. per month, with the going rate around 1/6d. per week.

On the farm the family had help from Edward Barlow and William Ward, both in their early twenties, who lived with the family, and regular, casual help from John Warbank who seems to have done some of the butchering, and intermittent help from others who came to do a specific job. Labour was also shared between the farms at Hatherton and Little Wyrley.

Sheep shearing was also another specialist job and in June 1840 there was a total of 37 fleeces.

In the house, the domestic help consisted of one female servant at any one time, Fanny Lovet, Ann Webb, E.Buttery and Charlotte Dean, none of them staying for long, and calling on another resident occasionally to wash blankets.

On the farming side of the business, Thomas would borrow pieces of machinery to suit his purpose, for example Mr. Masfen's drill to sow the wheat, Mr. Hawkins' machine for thrashing and winnowing the wheat over two days, plus two days at Little Wyrley, at a rate of 12/-d. per day, and a shilling for himself! Mr. Holmes' drill was used for sowing the peas, costing 2/6d., borrowing it again to sow the barley at Huntington, and this time the charge had risen to 3/-d. Mr. Wood from Rugeley provided his drill to sow the turnips at Mosswood and Little Wyrley.

A boat load of 20 tons of lime arrived via the canal at Wedges Mills, steered by W. Jackson, drawing 14 cart loads in 8 hours, which took two weeks to spread on the different fields. The farm horses, Gipsey, Merriman and Sharper, provided the transport for this work. They were also used to transport saleable crops to customers within the local area, for example taking wheat to Mr. Cotton the Miller at Cannock Mill. Coal was also transported from Brownhills, Forresters, Mr. Gilpin's, Brownhills Old Colliery, Churchbridge, Bakers of Wyrley Bank, Queens Colliery and Mr. Poyner's Coal Pits. The cost of a ton of coal was around 8s. and three loads from Brownhills £1.0.0d. This coal was also delivered to customers like Mrs. Knight, getting it in for her the following day.

Butchers provided "Fasting houses" in which animals intended for slaughter were kept for three days without food. Because of the bleating and moaning, these houses were kept far away from residents.

When harvest time drew near, long hours were worked, sometimes from 2.0a.m. until 11.0 p.m. and the next day "all were tiered from the dust". When it was time to thatch the large wheat rick, Thomas Anslow put his knife into the rick and lost it. As this incident was mentioned in the Diary, did it cause amusement or would the knife be an indispensable part of his trade, costing him money for a replacement he could ill afford to spend.

The family led a very active life within the community and father, being a "principle inhabitant of the town", was included in celebrations of the Queen's Coronation and subsequent marriage; the 21st birthday of the only son of Lord Hatherton, Edward Littleton, and also on his marriage.

Mrs. Walhouse of Hatherton Hall, and mother of Lord Hatherton, founded Walhouse School in Old Penkridge Road and was also a good friend and customer, and would invite the ladies of the family to drink tea with her, this being regarded as a social event. The women in the community took every opportunity to visit friends and neighbours to 'take tea'. Visits were regularly made to local people and the rest of the family within walking distance, relying on horse power to visit those who lived further away.

The Lindop family embraced their relatives visits, often putting them up for a day or two, or just providing them with a meal, although it is noted that visitors were more numerous in the summer weather, hampered by dark nights and bad weather during the winter. Visitors came from all over the locality, often bringing gifts with them such as cherries, gooseberries, apples, strawberries, greengages, nice pieces of fish and oysters, with most of them being extended family.

Members of the family attended Norton, Hatherton and Bloxwich Wakes and also the Races, held in August at Wolverhampton, Norton and Bloxwich, and July and October in Hednesford.

In existence was a Club for the ladies in Cannock and Norton, an Oyster Club for the men, and an Association Dinner was held in May. The Oyster Club was founded in Edinburgh in the middle half of the 19th century as a supper club for the 'literati' which allowed men of varied professions to meet, share ideas and laughs over dried salt haddock and oysters.

Tuesday May 5th 1840 saw the Association Dinner of the Tradesmen's association set up to protect against theft. It was started in Cannock in 1790 because of a lack of a police force. Each person paid yearly and then compensation was given to members suffering theft.

CRIME

By far the most sensational crime in the area at that time was the murder of Christina Collins at Rugeley, as seen elsewhere in the diary, which must have sent shock waves throughout Cannock Chase. This very serious crime was taken to Staffordshire Summer Assizes and did not come into the duties of "The Association".

By 1829 Robert Peel had founded the Metropolitan Police Force, a professional police force, needed to deal with the social turmoil of the 1830's with its threats to property and persons. "The Association" would be involved with local issues, for example:-

Mr. Bych's house of Leacroft was burgled and clothing taken.

Grandmother had 8 fowls and the Guinea cock stolen.

A sheep was stolen from J. G. Stubbs.

J. Lindop had 3 ducks stolen.

The Doctor was robbed of brandy.

5 hens and a Chinese cock were stolen from a hen roost, belonging to Mr. Henry Arthur of Cannock – the robbers were not found.

Thomas Hemmingsley and James Morris were charged with stealing one handkerchief, three half crowns and a sixpence in silver the property of John Smith of Norton Canes.
The hen roost belonging to Mrs. Massey of the Cross Keys, Hednesford was broken into and three couples of ducks and five couple of fowl were stolen. The thieves "have not been discovered as yet, but a reward is offered".

James Smith pleaded guilty to stealing a shirt of William Hill at Cannock – sentence two months.

Henry Wilkes was indicted for assaulting, stabbing and cutting Wm. Morgan. He stated that he was a sailor travelling to a sea port. The constable of Cannock was sent for to apprehend the prisoner on the night. On arriving at the spot he heard the prisoner say "I have stabbed the old bastard and I'll stab his heart out and I'll muzzle the constable if he puts his hands on me". Then he greatly resisted and was only arrested by the assistance of two other persons. The constable did not find anything on him, but found a knife in the Wolverhampton lock up. It was not there before the prisoner used the room. Mr. Henry Somerville, Surgeon of Cannock, stated that the wound inflicted on Morgan in the pit of his stomach was not a dangerous one, but was in a dangerous place. It would have required great force to have penetrated the liver.

Wilkes was given six months hard labour. The sentence was less severe than it could have been because Morgan had not attended the Court to prove the case. It could have been transportation.

On 20.8.1842 William Goodrich charged with killing and slaying Robert Lander at the parish of Cannock.

In January 1843 James Wall pleaded guilty to stealing five half pence, the property of Thomas Lindop of Norton Canes – imprisoned for four months once he had been privately whipped.

On 29.6.1841 Frederick Beaman aged 19 years was charged at his trial with stealing seven loaves of bread and two pieces of flannel, the property of John Ganderton at Cannock and committed to Stafford Gaol.

SHOPPING

Items necessary for day to day living were purchased locally and Cannock residents were more or less self sufficient. There were purchases made from the door as 'The Irishman' called, whereupon a pair of side combs were purchased, also from a caller, three lumps of salt, candles, isinglass, 1 lb. of tea and a tap. Other items were bag string, hair pins and Blares Pills 2s9d. from the stationers, for rhumatism "not to put hands into cold water when taking them".

Shoes and boots were bought locally from various boot and shoe makers and repaired frequently. New boots for George appear regularly and all was revealed on the 1841 Census, as George was four years old and, like all small children, had feet which kept getting bigger.

Mr. Biddle, a near neighbour and tailor, was given the job of making three black waistcoats, and from Mr. Smith of Norton a gross of pipes "for smoking" which cost 3.0d.

Mrs. Marshall the dressmaker was supplied with material to make a new frock, and on another occasion "new plaid" material costing 14s.9d. with the charge of 5s6d. for the dress to be made up. She also charged 2s 5½d. for trimming a new bonnet with ribbons. The Diary priced the new bonnets between 7s.4d. to £1.5s.0d. In comparison a book cost 16s.6d. a new pair of shoes 5s.6d. and four handkerchiefs 3s.6d.

Further afield, Sarah had a bonnet from Bloxwich, and from Wolverhampton on the shopping list were raisins 7½lb. Volatile Salts, cotton for a scarf, a 10 gallon saucepan, a poker and a shovel. Although they did a lot of their own brewing, they also purchased on the same shopping trip, a bottle of Port and Sherry wine costing 3s.9d. each.

Father and Thomas, the eldest son, on another trip to Wolverhampton, purchased a cap for both George and Thomas, a handkerchief for Sarah, some weights, a frock for Mary, a steel, and for the women a brooch for 4s.0d. and a necklace for 6s.0d.

When the family went to Stafford purchases included a warming pan, sugar nippers, a lid for the mustard pot, a new mustard pot, six good size goblets and a 'beautiful hyacinth'. It was also the opportunity to collect the cows and the cheese that all came from Chatcull and which had been resting at a half way house, somewhere near the town.

Apart from going into town, the family also made purchases from local farm sales, for example a slop bucket and eleven custard glasses from Mrs. Hall's Sale, furniture and other effects from the sale at Hemlock Farm belonging to Mrs. Marshall, a cow from Lord Hatherton's Sale and at Mr. N. Brookes Sale "a great many things".

Chatcull Old Hall Farm. A house has stood on this site since Doomsday.

The Sale was advertised thus:-

To Farmers, Malsters, Publican and Others – Sale at Norton Nr. Cannock by Farrington and Son, to be held by Auction on the premises on Friday July 31st 1840.

All the valuable stock of pale dried Malt, about 700 bushels, the property of the late Mr. N. Brookes, Farmer & Malster, in convenient lots to suit purchases. Sale to commence at 11 o'clock

Up until his death on 10th May, Mr. Brookes was brewing malt for Thomas Lindop, and he supplied the beef for his funeral.

At Miller's Sale at Otherton, a covered cart was purchased for £6.10.0d. and a wagon cloth for 8s.6d.

Lord Bishop of Lichfield held a Sale giving a chance to buy "a few of the famas potoeas that the Lord Bishop gave one guinea a peace for".

A SIGN OF THE TIMES

For the two years covered by the Diary the family seemed quite healthy, although George had measles, which at that time was considered serious, and Richard was taken poorly a couple of months later. Father suffered from toothache, using Salomonia drops, and two teaspoonful of Sweet Spirit of Vitre. Mother was poorly and had to send for the Doctor just a week before Christmas, with Aunt Jane, mother's sister, helping to look after her and the family.

One family in the area were all ill with small pox, although the mother was not affected.

When illness appeared, very often death was not far away, with age no barrier. The father of one family died leaving four children, and his wife "in the family way". How would the family cope with the breadwinner no longer there?

On 9th May 1840 Mrs. G. Hawkes, wife of Rev. Hawkes of Norton Hall, gave birth to a daughter and on 5th February 1841 gave birth to another daughter. In March Mother visited them and was "very pleased", taking with her some cake to give the children. On 3rd August 1842 Mrs. Hawkes was confined of another daughter at one o'clock and died at 7.0 a.m. aged 36 years. It is wondered if the baby survived. This was a situation replicated throughout the country at this time.

Fanny Lindop, grandmother from Chatcull appears to be a money lender, as payments from relatives are made to her at £3.0.0d. for one year's interest. It was quite common at this time for women with a little capital to lend money, particularly if they were living on their own.

During the two years covered by the Diary there were two fires, one at Mr. Silvester's farm at Little Wyrley in April 1840 which burnt all the hay, two hovels and the cow shed, caused by the housemaid carrying hot ashes, and in June 1841 Mrs. Barlow had a fire at her home at Chatcull. Because one of the chimneys having fallen on the thatch the house was entirely destroyed, together with a large proportion of furniture, malt and cheese. Did the new fire engine attend either of these fires? If you had no fire premium it was not obliged to attend.

EVENTS

Although Cannock was at this time a quiet market town, situations occurred which would have caused speculation with the community. Apart from crime, accidents would have been of major interest. The family were regular subscribers to The Staffordshire Advertiser, costing four and a half pence or 5s.3d. per quarter, so would be well informed about local news. They also purchased books, not common amongst the ordinary working man, enabling them to enter into intelligent debate.

Mr. Davison, Auctioneer, Surveyor, Land Agent, had a fatal accident when he was thrown out of a spring cart (full report in the Diary).

In June 1840, as reported in the newspaper, Mr. Fry, Surgeon of Cannock, was returning from Brewood in a small pony carriage, when from some unknown cause, the pony took fright and threw him out, fracturing both legs and dislocating his hip. Prior to this he was thrown from his horse, breaking his thigh, preventing him from riding on horseback. Mr. Fry left Cannock in March1841.

Richard Simms, an agricultural labourer, living at the farm at Little Wyrley, twenty two years of age, died of suffocation in a barn at Norton. Whilst sleeping there, a cart load of barley fell upon him and he could not be pulled clear quickly enough to save his life.

Fredk. Pratt became quite a celebrity when, for a wager, rode a horse in February for twenty miles in less than one hour (see Diary).

In November 1840 "the balloon passed through and dropped near the Crosses, it came from West Bromwich". The impression is that the children chased it, taking a short cut, and were able to try it out.

Accidents on the farm could occasionally happen causing considerable concern, as when "W. Sothens ketched the wall at the Barn on the left and side, and sent it all down, and the door as well – thanks be to God that no one was hert".

The well-known celebrity at that time, the Most Honourable Henry William, Marquis of Anglesey, attended the Court at the Crown Hotel, Cannock.

TRANSPORT AND TRAVEL

Pre 1830 the movement of people, goods and animals, would have been restricted to canals, built in the late 1700's, horse and cart, stage coach and by foot. This influenced movement and distance travelled. However, by 1836 the "raleroad" from London to Liverpool and Manchester had been constructed, the cutting edge technology of the day. The train stopped at Penkridge and Stafford among many other towns, giving access for local people.

In February 1840 Lord Hatherton wrote in his diary "By the railroad to Teddesley, reached Penkridge in six hours, having set down by a first class train. Lord Stanley and many other Members on the train". During March 1840 "Went to Teddesley by the rail and arrived (in London) half past three. Such despatches will be familiar to the next generation – but to me, who remembers a two day long journey to Town (London) it is wonderful". What a difference it would make to him, travelling to London on a frequent basis to sit in the House of Lords.

A major bridge was built by the world famous civil engineer Thomas Brassey at Penkridge, surviving to this day.

It is wondered what local people thought of this revolution, as some people were frightened to use the 'railroad' fearing that illness would attack them after travelling at the great speed of 30mph.

Our Lindop family seemed quite prepared to use this new facility, as Father took the Vicar to the station at the Spread Eagle because he was leaving Cannock for another Parish. In another instance Ann Lindop from Milton was being met by her brother at Penkridge coming "by the rale road".

Thomas Brassey, apart from building bridges, was also busy constructing new improved roads, making it easier to travel with more comfort.

Another method of travel was by canal at Churchbridge, used for the transportation of coal, and in particular lime by the ton to spread on the fields. It was also used to carry people, as can be seen in the Christina Collins murder, with particular boats called 'Flyers' using more speed, although by 1840 the trains were proving to be a much more comfortable and faster form of travel.

RELIGIOUS CELEBRATIONS

Attending Church is only mentioned occasionally and then it is the younger members of the family who attend with Grandmother, although there are frequent references to the past and present Vicars, and the subject of their sermons. As they lived close by St. Luke's Church, perhaps attending the services was so routine that there was no need to mention this activity in the Diary.

Good Friday appears to be the day that had a special significance, as for both years on

17th April 1840 and 9th April 1841, lambs born late in February were killed on those days. Lambs were also killed for Mrs. Walhouse, Mr. Sheriden and Mr. Masfin. There is no mention in the diary of attending church on Easter Sunday for either year.

During Christmas 1840 Mother had been ill enough for the Doctor to be called in and she was still in bed on Christmas Day. However she made the effort later in the day to go to Wyrley but was "very poorly" when she arrived. Was she determined to visit her mother?

It is known that Christmas was not celebrated as we know it until a few years into Queen Victoria's reign. As she was married in 1840 it was not until she had family that more celebration was made of Christmas. Prince Albert introduced the Christmas Tree, which has remained part of the tradition to this day.

THE RACES

The family were keen race goers, attending most of the local races, although when Mr. J. Wright of Wolverhampton sent his cousin J. Phillips Wright to take Sarah to the races "her Father did not wish her to go".

They went to Norton and Bloxwich Races in August and Hednesford Races in October, one course being 'the birch tree course'. They enjoyed this sporting activity so much that one member of the family was 'very tipsy'.

Wolverhampton Races on 12th August 1841 "the sport on Monday was usually of good character. The rain which fell in torrents on Tuesday evening and the following morning made the ground exceedingly heavy. The company was not so numerous as on the proceeding days. On arriving at the winner's chair the horses were so besmattered with mud as to render their colours in front scarely distinguishable" the *Staffordshire Advertiser* reports.

EXPENSES

Land Tithes of 1843 – Thomas Lindop paid out rents to various owners of land as follows:-

Samuel Barber	£1. 1. 4d.
Rev. Robert Baxter	£1. 1. 10d.
Rev. S. Clavering	£1. 3. 10d.
Ann Hand	£0. 4. 9d.
Dorothy Rye	£1. 1. 3d.
T.C. Savage	£4. 6. 10d.
T. Lindop	£3. 6. 10d.

Some of the farm was part of Lord Hatherton's Estate and once a year a visit was made to Walsall to pay the rent of £21.5.0d.
A road survey had to be paid and 1s.6d. for the Turnpike road.
Church rate 7s.6½d.

Land Tax 14s.0d.

Fire Office premium 4s.0d. per year.

The Staffordshire Advertiser £1. 1s. 0d. for the year.

Towards the fresh clergy 10s.0d.

Another set of Church Rates 12s.11½d.

Stones for the road 5s.0d.

Church Rate:: could be the stipend paid to the curate. Each churchgoer would be expected to pay a certain amount.

To balance these expenses he received from his various tenants 1s.6d. per week on average.

FAIRS

Thomas Lindop attended most of the local Fairs, enabling him to buy and sell his animals.

11th January 1841 Monday was the first fortnightly cattle market at Stafford, also held at Fazeley and Newcastle New Market.

12th January 1841 Tuesday markets at Shrewsbury.

13th January 1841 Wednesday markets at Dunchurch, Lichfield and Uttoxeter.

In October at Stafford Cheese Fair a considerable quantity of cheese was pitched, which met with ready sale at good prices. Prime dairies raised from 63s. to 65s. per cwt.

In May a Fair where sheep, cattle and horses were sold.

Lichfield also held a May Fair and was pretty well supplied with cattle, and prices were beef 7d. per lb. and mutton 7½d. Store stock fetched very high prices and a good many were penned. "Of cheese and bacon there was a moderate supply with cheese averaging 70s. per cwt. with bacon and hams 7½ – 8½ lbs in weight".

Wolverhampton held a weekly market on a Wednesday and Rugeley Great Horse Fair was held on 3rd to 8th of June and during the year a ploughing match was held.

Rugeley Annual Cattle Show was held on 5.12.1840 in the spacious yard at the Talbot Arms Inn at l0.00 o'clock. "The Annual Dinner to commemorate the 11th Anniversary of its establishment will take place after the show. Jame O. Oldham Esq. of Bellamore Hall has accepted an invitation to preside on the occasion. From the increasing interest taken in this cattle show, it is expected that the attendance will be both numerous and respectable".

OLD HALL FARM, CHATCULL – Owned by the Swinfen Jervis family

The family seems to have begun in Chatkyll with James Jervis of Chatkyll who had two sons, Robert who lived at Chatkyll and William who lived at Ollerton. Robert had a son, John Jervis born in 1599 and who was buried at Eccleshall in 1670. His son, also John, was born at Standon in September 1631 and was buried at Eccleshall in 1680. He married Elizabeth, daughter of Robert Wakelin of Gentleshaw in the parish of Longdon. They had a son John born at Chatkyll and buried at Darlaston. He married Mary, daughter and heiress of John Swynfen. They had six sons, the fifth being Swynfen Jervis who was born at Darlaston in 1700. He later moved to Meaford near Stone. He married Elizabeth Parker of Park Hall and they had William Jervis born in 1728. More importantly to English History their other son, John, was to become an Admiral in the Fleet.

He along with Admiral Grey took part in the infamous West Indies Campaign. During it they took various islands from the French, including Martinique and Guadaloupe, before losing them again. Grey at the time was accused of cowardice. Jervis went on to defeat the Spanish at the Battle of Cape St. Vincent and was honoured with a peerage, becoming Earl St. Vincent.

The farm which the Lindops rented was owned by descendents of the Jervis family.

Although the three sons, Joseph, Richard and Thomas Lindop, had left the family at Chatcull to take farms at Little Wyrley, Hatherton and Cannock, it was still a meeting place, especially for the men of the family, and where money was borrowed from Grandmother and paid back with interest.

A stay overnight was quite usual, distance being the problem, and when cows, sheep, lambs and large quantities of cheese were exchanging hands, somewhere in Stafford would be the half-way meeting point. Eliza, their daughter, married William Summerfield and they were regular visitors.

By 1840 Frances had been a widow for 35 years and so middle son John, aged 45 years, took over the running of the farm together with his wife Mary and their eight children. It is thought that Mary their aunt was also at the farm. Frances, Fanny as she was known, was by this time 75 years old. Livestock was still being brought from there and cheese was being made in large quantities.

There were, and still are, few properties in Chatcull.

NOTABLE PEOPLE IN THE AREA

First and foremost would be the Earl of Uxbridge and Lord Hatherton of Teddesley Hall.

Mrs. Walhouse, mother of Lord Hatherton, wife of Moreton Walhouse, lived at Hatherton Hall. She had a great influence in Cannock, founding and supporting Walhouse School in Old Penkridge Road. The school was built by Edward Birch in 1828, brother to the old parish clerk. Both Mrs. Walhouse and her two daughters took great interest in the whole undertaking, acting as teachers one or two mornings a week and invariably on Sunday morning being driven to school in her carriage, drawn by a pair of horses, with coachman and footman, who returned to Hatherton Hall till the closing of the morning school, when the carriage would return to take them home, or to Cannock Church. She was a good customer of the Lindop family and occasionally the women of the family would take tea with her.

Phineas Fowke Hussey Esq., Lord of the Manor of Little Wyrley, baptised 16.1.1822 died 30.10.1867 at St. James Church, Norton Canes. His father Phineas, mother Sophia. The family were in Norton since the early 1700's – father was a Hussey and mother a Fowke. Father died in January 1833 leaving debts of £5395. The family had interests in both the Brownhills Colliery and the local canals.

The Rev. G. J. Hawkes, lived at Norton Hall.

William Masfen and his son Joseph. William, amongst other activities was Treasurer of the Conduit Trust.

William Gilpin coal merchant and iron master.

William Henry Stubbs and family of Bitterton.

Rev. W. B. Collis, priest in charge at St. Lukes between 1802 – 1811 and when retired, returned to Cannock.

Mrs. Sarah Knight of independent means, a close neighbour and friend aged 75 years; her daughter Mary aged 45 years and Ann Hodson, domestic aged 30 years lived with her Thomas Sant and son Edward, lived in Mill Street.

Mr. Poyner, next door neighbour and farmer.

George Tomlinson builder.

Mr. Biddle, a near neighbour and tailor.

Mr. Cope who had a drapery business.

Mr. Hanbury lived at Leacroft.

Most of the above being members of the Conduit Trust.

A hundred years earlier the only supply of water for Cannock, with its 365 people from 91 households, was from natural springs, streams or rivers, with a few, who could afford to sink a well.

This was to change when Dr. William Byrche, Chancellor of the Diocese of Worcester and owner of Leacroft Hall, decided that as his land at Leacroft covered Stringers Meadow in Rumer Hill with a natural spring. He decided to lay a conduit from the spring into

Cannock, with the main head and pump sited close to the Bowling Green, providing the townspeople with clean, safe drinking water. In time pumps were installed in Mill Street near to the Yew Tree Inn, High Green, the junction of Old Penkridge Road and Hatherton Road, near the Smithy in Walsall Road, the junction between Mill Street and Price Street, and one in the town centre opposite the Crown Hotel.

The scheme was named "The Conduit Trust" and several of the Trustees were men mentioned in the Diary. It is taken for granted now to have an endless supply of safe water, but in 1840/1841 the community would have daily fetched their water from one of the six pumps

A full story on the Conduit Trust can be found in the book *"Cannock Town Centre Through The Ages"* published November 2004.

The Old Conduit House, Cannock.

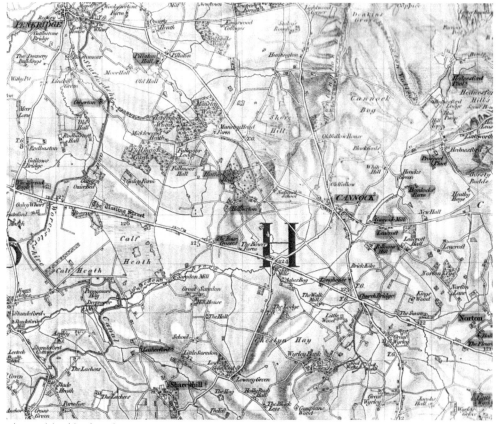

Places visited in the Diary.

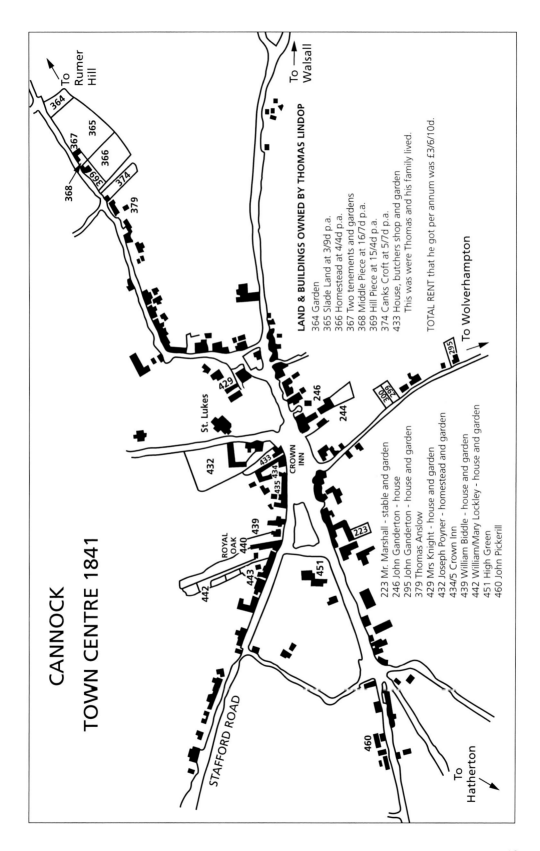

CANNOCK
TOWN CENTRE 1841

To Rumer Hill

To Walsall

St. Lukes

CROWN INN

ROYAL OAK

STAFFORD ROAD

To Wolverhampton

To Hatherton

LAND & BUILDINGS OWNED BY THOMAS LINDOP

364 Garden
365 Slade Land at 3/9d p.a.
366 Homestead at 4/4d p.a.
367 Two tenements and gardens
368 Middle Piece at 16/7d p.a.
369 Hill Piece at 15/4d p.a.
374 Canks Croft at 5/7d p.a.
433 House, butchers shop and garden
     This was were Thomas and his family lived.

TOTAL RENT that he got per annum was £3/6/10d.

223 Mr. Marshall - stable and garden
246 John Ganderton - house
295 John Ganderton - house and garden
379 Thomas Anslow
429 Mrs Knight - house and garden
432 Joseph Poyner - homestead and garden
434/5 Crown Inn
439 William Biddle - house and garden
442 William/Mary Lockley - house and garden
451 High Green
460 John Pickerill

Mary Lindop's Diary

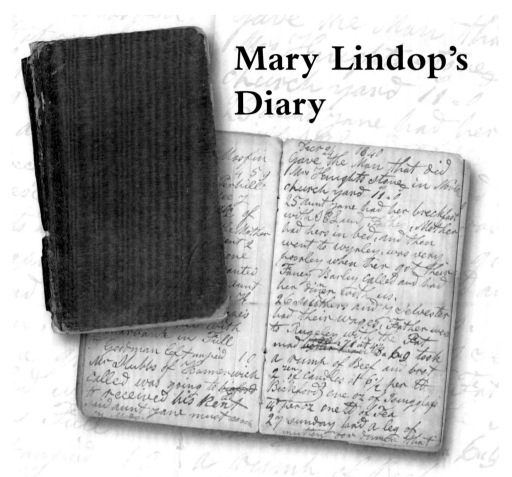

* **Please remember that when reading the diary I have kept to Mary Lindop's original spelling which appears in serif type style.** Any research and additions appear in a sans serif type style and information in brackets refers to links in various parts of the diary.

1838

HOW CANNOCK CELEBRATED THE CORONATION IN 1838

The following are extracts from a reprint of the *"Staffordshire Advertiser"*:

At Cannock, the morning of this August an all interesting ceremony was ushered in by merry peals of the village bells, the band playing their favourite airs. At half past one o'clock upwards of a 1000 of the poor of the village and its vicinity partook of a good dinner of roast beef, plum pudding, and of a large sheep roasted whole, with an ample supply of ale etc. Dinners were attended afterwards by the principle inhabitants at the different inns, which were presided over by W. L. Gilpin Esq. and the Rev W. B. Collis, as chairman; G. Hawkes Esq., of Norton Hall, and T. Holmes Esq; officiating as vice chairman. Many animating and patriotic speeches were delivered, and the best and most loyal feeling universally pervaded each assembly. On Friday evening between three and four hundred persons, consisting of the ladies and other respectable female inhabitants of the village and neighbourhood, drank tea together in a large room fitted up for the occasion. After tea they walked in procession through the village, preceded by the band, and followed by the gentlemen. Arriving at the Bowling Green, they formed themselves into a large square, the band occupying an elevated situation in the centre, and with manifestations of feeling which it is impossible to describe, sang the National Anthem, which was followed with three hearty cheers of the most deafening description. They then joined in the merry dance, keeping it up with spirit till eleven o'clock when they peaceably separated for their respective homes, delighted with the harmonious enjoyments of the evening, sincerely wishing health, happiness, and long life to their beloved Queen, and that a reign so auspiciously began might be the harbinger of increasing national prosperity.

Cannock Wind Team Band consisted of Mr. Robert Masfen senior one of the founders. He was quite a competent musician as he received instructions from a military bandmaster so that he could put at the disposal of the Cannock band his experience and ability. The band then consisted of Robert Masfen, Edward Sant junior a member of a very ancient Cannock family, Dr. Field a well known Cannock physician. Other members were John Cooke drummer and bass singer, William Birch French horn and bass singer, Thomas Hill French horn and bass singer, Edward Birch clarinet and tenor singer, Thomas Stringer French horn and alto singer, John Stringer bass trombone, John Rochell trumpet, John Benton clarinet, William Benton clarinet and leader, John Trubshaw serpent in brass instrument, Joe Trubshaw clarinet, Robert Bailey bassoon, Edward Thomas serpent, Parish Clerk Birch trumpet, John Corns triangle, John Chackett, George Thomas, William Biddle bassoon, Joseph Bick oboe, Joseph Urpe bassoon, James Brooks clarinet- a total of 24 members. (Information from Recollection of old Cannock. *Cannock Advertiser*)

This band also played for services in St. Luke's Parish Church, prior to an organ being installed.

1839

4th December

Father went to Stafford fair

January:- Monday Jan. 11th was the first fortnightly cattle market at Stafford. Also held at Fazeley and Newcastle new market.

Jan 12th. Held at Shrewsbury. Jan 13th held at Dunchurch, Lichfield and Uttoxeter.

May:- Lichfield pretty well supplied with cattle. Prices were beef 7d per lb and mutton 7 and a half pence. Store stock fetched very high prices.

Lichfield annual May fair- a good many cattle they were penned. "Of cheese and bacon there was a moderate supply. Cheese averaged about 70s. per cwt; bacon and hams from 7 and a half to 8 and a half lbs in weight.

October:- Stafford cheese fair- At our autumnal cheese fair on Monday October 4th a considerable quantity of cheese was pitched which met with ready sale at good prices. Prime dairies ranged from 63s. to 65s. per cwt.

5th December

Killed a pig

6th December

Went to Stafford (over the weights 15:61/2)

9th December

Father went to Fazeley and bought a fat cow of Mr. Booth for £28 or	**£26 15s 0d**
There was a fortnightly cattle market there.	

A cow of Mr. Smith of Norton	**£5 15s 0d**
John Smith farmer.	

Give Mr. Bailey for Mr. Shield	**5s 0d**
John Bailey, a 75 year old agricultural labourer who lived in Cannock. Mr Shield might be a misspelling for Sheil (John) the curate, aged 60.	

10th December

Went to Rugeley and Teddesley and bought two pigs

11th December

Went to Wolverhampton and received a hare a brace of Pheasants a ditto Rabbits
Of Lord Hatherton

Written along the right hand side of the diary – **It is the Lord, let him do what seemeth him good (San 111:13)**

My Mother is 75 years old in October 1846

Can only be Mary Walker, her grandmother, who was registered as 70 on the 1841 census.

12th December

Went to Wyrley and Mr. Shorters

Mary's older sister Sarah Eliza marries James Shorter on July 5th 1843. He died on 19-11-46 aged just 27. His father was William Shorter who lived at Cheslyn Hay in Cheslyn Hay House. He died 4-8-42 aged 50.

Bought a calf of Mrs. Walhouse

15th December

Paid Mrs. Lindop of Hatherton (sister-in-law)	**£41 0s 0d**
Mary Lindop married to Richard Lindop (deceased), Thomas's brother. She lived with her family.	

16thDecember

Went to Wyrley (Little Wyrley)

17th December

Killed the Cow has come from Dunston

18th December

Killed the Cow has come from Fazeley and the small pig
from Teddesley

19th December

Killed the large pig from Tedlery (Teddesley) and the cow
at Hatherton

20th December

Cut the beef up and the Cow at Hatherton

Market Square, Cannock.

(Written on the side) the incumbency Cannock 1842 has
been presented ~Dean & Chapter to the Rev. F. (Francis) T.
Blackburne, curate Harborne the first text that I herd him
give was – My Grace is sufficient for thee.

Cut two of Mr. Masfin's sheep up a Leicestershire and a Cannock Wood	6.0d
The little one	12.9d
The large one	3. 5d
The fat pig that has come from Teddesley weighed by Mr. Collis (vicar of Cannock)	3. 5d

Mr. Jening road servey	0 3d

Paid W. Smith coal bill 6s 7d

William Smith was a farmer living at Long House, down near today's Delta Way. Longhouse Farm Colliery, also known as Waterloo Colliery, had been opened by Joseph Palmer junior, brother to William Palmer, the Rugeley poisoner, after he leased land from Lord Hatherton in the 1830's. Small mine with only two shafts, each about 90 yards deep.
*see also 6-2-40

Mr. Jening road sevey 0.8d

Setled with Miss Horden on the first of Jan.1840

Mary Horden an independant lady aged 65 living in Cannock.

1840

1st January

Ward came (aged 22 – labourer living in)

2nd January

Fetched Mrs. Carr's calf 3s 0d

Elizabeth Carr who lived at the Hazel Slade stables which her son, Thomas, ran them when her son died in 1847. She left and went to live with her daughter at Longdon. She died in 1852 aged 80.

Jack came found a Hair in the Garden caught by a wire

Bought of (S) ~Wright) 4 sheep at 6¾ Per lb

Farmer near Wolverhampton?

Weighed one sheep of R. W.B. Collis (Vicar of Cannock) 94 lb.

Ward fetched a wagon load of coals from Brownhills 13s 10d

Most likely the conduit mines run by William Hanbury which he had originally leased from the Hussey family. *More in miners book pp.188/89.

W. Southern (William) came to Wyrley (aged 25 Ag. Lab)

Worked for John Sylvester, aged 40, a farmer at Little Wyrley. Thomas's brother, Joseph, had married Elizabeth Sylvester on Aug 27th 1816.

3rd January

Killed Mrs. Carr's calf 44 lbs.

S. Wright sheep killed

Mr. Knights coals 5s 11d

Mrs Knight's son?

Paid J. Smith for shoes for J. & R. (Richard) 18s 0d

> He had taken over the business from his father, Samuel, who had it in
> 1834 (*White's Directory*).

7th January

Killed one Mr. Wright 71 lbs. Sheep

Grandmother went to Wyrley I came back from Wyrley

> Mary Walker, aged 70, who had a farm there.

9th January

Killed a red cow of Mr. B. And one of our sheep

**S.E.L. and T.L. (Sarah & Thomas) went to Mr. Chamberlins-
Fordhouses (see 12.1.40)**

10th January

Went to settle with JS took for Mr. Cotton to Mr. N.B.

Found him at Mr. Jenneys the men fetching lime (see 28.12.39)

> John Smith of Norton. Mr. Cotton is the mill owner. N.B is Nathaniel
> Brookes a farmer at Norton and Mr. Jenney is James Jenney of Norton.

11th January

Gave (J) Selvester brother (John Silvester ag. Lab. Little Wyrley) 2.0d

Paid Mr. Wright Wolverhampton 6.10.0d

Mary Perrens (tenant) paid 4.0d

13th January

Mr. Davinson was thrown out of a spring cart and killed on Wendesday night

> Report from *The Staffordshire Advertiser* of January 11th 1840-
> Mr. James Davison, aged 36 of Forebridge, Stafford, auctioneer,
> surveyor and land agent was at Mr. Robinson's preparing an inventory
> of his stock prior to sale. Mr. Davison's death was occasioned by
> his being thrown out of a light spring cart, on his return from Mr.
> Robinson's of the Lower Heamies Nr. Eccleshall. He left Mr. Robinson's
> about 10 o'clock at night, in his spring cart drawn by a spirited pony,
> taking with him one of Mr. Robinson's men with a lanthorn, the night
> being extremely dark. About a mile from the house, at a sharp turn,
> where a gutter runs across the lane. Mr. Davison was thrown out, the
> reins falling, the pony ran away. Mr. Davison was found insensible
> and speechless. The man with him was unhurt and he obtained the
> assistance of a labourer from Mr. Halls but before they could bring the
> cart and pony back Mr. Davison had ceased to breath, a surgeon was
> sent for but no use. A verdict of accidental death. Mr. Davison was

known as a skilful surveyor and soundness of judgement as a valuer and appraiser, and was perhaps excelled by a few.

His father Mr. Henry Davison advertised in the paper that he would carry on his son's business to support his widow and children.

In the same month it was reported in *The Staffordshire Advertiser* the death of Alexander Stewart, infant son of the late James Davison.

27-6-40- A lamentable accident occurred to Mr. Fry surgeon of Cannock, as he was returning from Brewood in a small pony carriage on Friday. From some unknown cause the pony took fright and threw the unfortunate gentleman out and fractured both his legs and dislocated his hip. What makes the accident singularly unfortunate is that some time ago Mr. Fry was thrown from his horse and broke his thigh which prevented him from riding on horseback. Mr. Fry left Cannock on 18th March 1841.

12 January

Sent Jack S---r to fetch Sarah and Thomas from Mr. Woods and was not come from the fordhouses.

Jack S is James Sylvester ag. labourer living at Hatherton aged 55.

Mr. Bych's houses of Leacroft was entered last night through the room winder clothing taken

Received yesterday Mrs. Walhouse check

Paid Mr. Hall today(shoemaker)

Received of J. Darbey   1s 6d
Tenant who lived in Mill Street.

13th January

Heard as Uncle William was ill. (see 14.1.40)

Uncle William is Thomas's older brother who lived at Milton.

Mrs. Walhouse gave us a haire

Richard went to Mr. Walmsley

Bought Mr. Poyner's sheep – 20 at 7 per hand – 10.0s. Back

Mr. Poyner was a farmer, aged 40, who owned the property next door to Thomas in Cannock *See map.

Mr. Brown called from Wolverhampton

Bought the Poney of Mr. Holland   £9 10 0d

> Mr. Holland (Trevor Latham) was a surgeon who had been in Cannock some years. Dr. Holland was an apprentice to Dr. Field. Holland was known and dreaded by school children in the Parish , his delight was in having a prancing horse with which he would make children he met on their way from school flee to the first gate or gap in the hedge for safety.

Sent Mr. Jewewine book over (see 19.1.40)

SEL and TL came back (from Fordhouses – see 9.1.40)

14th January

Mr. Jendwine paid is account (Vicar)   £2 2s 7d

Father & Unle Joseph went to see Uncle William (Milton)
see 13.2.40

Paid W. Bailey for M.L. shoes (Mary Lindop aged 12)   1s 4d
> W.Bailey is a Cannock shopkeeper.

Set the Hen at the Barn

15th January

Washing Soda 3d lb.

Returned from Milton (see 14. 2.40) not Chatcull but Milton

Father found Uncle better had a fair day

16th January

Mrs. Wood and E.(?) otton (could be Cotton) came

Received of Price   £1.0s.0d

Fetched 3 of M. Poyners sheep

Settled with Mr. Stokes
> Mr. Stokes was a farmer at Leacroft.

17th January

T.L. Went to Wyrley (Thomas Lindop age 13 yrs)

Killed 3 of Mr. Poyners sheep (see above)

18th January

Weighed 3 of -------?

Mrs. P sent a Pork pie
> Mrs. P- could be Mrs Poyner.

Fire Ingen passed through

Teddesley Hall, Penkridge.

On Feb 3rd. Lord Hatherton,s Diary –Saw the fire Engine at Penkridge. There is a great rivalry now between the Birmingham and the District Fire Company in this neighbourhood. The B. Co. insisted in the Stafford paper that they were about to send an engine to be permanently stationed at Penkridge, and which the D.Co. actually sent one – which was immediately brought to Teddesley. Meantime a Paper War is going on between the Agents of the two Companies at Penkridge, who are rival forces in the town – one of whom, the weaker in popularity of the two has used my name unsatisfactorily in the warfare.

The Staffordshire Advertiser - 15.2.40
The directors most respectfully inform the Nobility, Gentry and inhabitants of Penkridge and its vicinity, that they forwarded on Saturday last a SUPERIOR NEW FIRE ENGINE for the better protection of their friends and the public generally and in acknowledging the constant and steady support afforded them for 35 years past, beg to assume them their practice in future be guided by the same just and honourable principles which have characterised their management on all occasions.

Paid Mr. Alsopp for seed wheat – 12 bushel at 10s.

Mr. Alsopp- Joseph Alsopp a farmer at Gailey aged 55.

Bought a lump of salt

£6 0s 0d

Brought a parcel of Box   1s 0d.

Fetched one sheep from Mr. Wrights weighed 50 lb.

An Extraordinary high Wind

21st January

Began the Hedge at the common Field

Went to Wolverhampton

> A charter conferred rights to
> Wolverhampton to hold a weekly market
> on a Wednesday and an annual fair on
> the eve of St.Peter and Paul's (June 29th).
> It was held from as long as 1204. It was
> held in Queen Square. Explains why
> father goes to W'ton on Wednesdays.

22nd January

Mother and Sister and Father – bought S.E.L. Boea(?) and
F black cravat and scarlet handkerchief

Brewed 3 Strike of Malt from Mr. H. – herd that F. Cappell taken

23rd January

Killed 2 Mr. Poyners sheep

24th January

Sould the last cheese (see 7.2.40)

Supt with Mr. Hubert for the first time

Setled with R. Whitehouse

25th January

John Darby paid (tenant)

John Silvester cash (ag.lab. aged 15 yrs. Little Wyrley)   1s 0d

26th January

A fresh Clergyman	1s 0d

Emma Buttery cash

27th January

Killed one of our cows and one of P----sheep	3s 6d

Bought G. L. Boots (George Lindop aged 5 years)

Hatherton Hall.

Went to Hatherton Hall after 7 o'clock one Mrs. Dawson account (Mrs. Walhouse's Housekeeper)

Went to Walsall to pay the rent

28th January

Bought 2 bols of bag string	£21 5s 0d
Brought the Hay into the Yard	11d

29th January

Sold the poney R. Toft - bought 2 bookes - one peney of hare pins

30th January

Sent 49 bags of wheat to Mr. Cotton

31st January

Killed 2 Mr. P---- sheep – gave Sutherns 5.0d.
(William Southerns aged 25 ag.lab. Little Wyrley)

Mr. Brookes gave us an Haire

Setled with Mrs. Marshall of Hemlocks (see 4.2.40)

1st February

E. Par---- called on the 29th Jan

R. Jesson Esq. Died in is 32nd year of his age

Received of John Darby

Mrs. Marshall died the druges?   1s 6d

2nd February

Mary Perrins paid 2.0d. – owes 4.0d. Up tow day

3rd February

Mrs. Marshall sale today (Hemlocks?)

Mrs. Collis of Hemlock (see 1.2.40)

4th February

Sold Furniture and other Effects

Killed a pig from Mr. Cottons for Mrs. Knight, J. Warbank helped, killed one of our own
   Mr. Cotton of Pillarton Hall Farm.

the weight of Mr. Cotton Pig for Mrs. Knight 318 lb. – had a side of ours and let Mr. Sant of a side of Mr. Cotton. Mrs. Knight 282 Mr. Sant 145

5th February

Setled with W.B. Collis

Went with Mr. Sheridan to Lord Bishop of Lichfield Sale

6th February

William for coals from smith (William Ward)

Turnpike   18s 4d

Put two Mr. P---- sheep   1s 6d

Went from the sale at Lichfield to Chatcull

Bot two cows of J. Lindop of Chatcull (see 11.2.40)
  J. Lindop- John, Thomas's younger brother, who is running the farm
  for their mother.

7th February

Bout Cheese 3.3.0 per Hun   £16 1s 0d

Brot a few of the famas potoeas that the Lord Bishop gave
one guinea a for

Brot one cheese with them (see 24.1.40)

Went to supper at the Crown

Market Place, Cannock.

Setled with Mr. Brinley
Mr. Brindley a wheelwright or Edward Brindley who lived
at the four crosses and was a bailiff aged 30.

8th February

Setled with Miss H. Hilpin

W. Stubbs called of H-land

Sent for Mr. Brinley to settle

Mary Perrens paid 2/-d. Owes 3/-d.

9th February

Blares Pills 2.9d. Per box to be got at the Stationers – not to put your hands into cold water when takin them for the Rumatisam

Received of Mr. Price

10th February

Paid Mr. Shaw for Go plough Back and reans	£1 0s 0d
New reans	£1 0s 0d
The Queen married	7s 6d

MARRIAGE OF HER MAJESTY QUEEN VICTORIA TO PRINCE ALBERT as reported in the Standard on Monday. The august and interesting ceremony of the marriage of her Most Gracious Majesty Queen Victoria, with his Royal Highness Prince Albert, of Saxe Coburg and Gotha was performed, announced, in the Chapel Royal, St. James's Palace. An event so novel as this, more that a century having elapsed since the nuptials of a reigning Queen of this country were celebrated, would be sufficient, independent of the magnificence and splendour attendant thereon, and the youth of our beloved Sovereign, to engage the universal attention and interest of the Nation. It is not then, to be wondered at that these combined circumstances should make the people of this Country who are, despite what a disaffected few may say, or think, naturally and intrinsically a royal people, suspend their ordinary avocations and cease their labouring toil, to join in keeping holiday, and publicly to demonstrate their attachment to the Throne and their earnest wishes for the welfare and happiness of their young and lovely Queen. – In Cannock 'Father dining at the Crown to honour the Queen's weeding' In *Lord Hatherton's Diary* it is noted – 'The Queen's Wedding - £70 collected in Penkridge for beef given in just proportions to the labourers. The school children arrived for tea and cake. I gave beef to all my own labourers not residing in Penkridge Parish. The principle tenants dined together at the Littleton Arms.

Report from the *Staffordshire Advertiser*-
The day of the Royal Nuptials was celebrated at Cannock by a public dinner at the Crown Inn, which was attended by most of the respectable inhabitants. The Chair was occupied by W. Gilpin Esq. of Wedges Mills who distributed during the late severe winter his annual and munificent Christmas benefit of 120 tonnes of coal among the poor of Cannock, and H. Sommerville Esq. officiated as vice chairman. The leading toasts of the day were drunk with great enthusiasm and the afternoon was one of unmingled enjoyment. In the evening the house of Mr. Thomas Baynbarn, officer of excise, was illuminated and a handsome figure of the Queen splendidly attired was exhibited in one of the windows.

11th February

Fetched two cows from Stafford – met Mr. J. Lindop they was is cows (see 7.2.40)

W. Brown called herd that W. Lindop (William) was worse (14.1.40)

12th February

Bought one cowe of Mr. Tomlinson

Killed Mr. Wright sheep

Betty Darby paid

Took Gipsey to Wyrley to fetch coals
Gipsy is the name of the pony.

Fetch the colt up today   1s 6d

13th February

Mr. Wright sheep 50 lb.

The man came to tell that Uncle William was dead
(William Lindop see (11.2.40)

Killed one pig at Wyrley – J. Warbank helpt to kill it

Joseph Moesley called and said he had left the fordhouses (12.1.40)

14th February

Killed 2 of Mr. P---- sheep

Went to Uncle Williams funeral

Grave of William Lindop late of Salt Hall who died at Milton, February 1840 aged 56.

15th February

Betty Darbey
Came back from the funeral at half past nine o'clock at night,
a very wet day Uncle William aged 56 (14.2.40 – could have
stayed overnight

16th February

Sunday Uncle Somerfield and Uncle James Lindop came back
(from the funeral?) – left R.L. at Chatcull (Richard Lindop)   1s 6d
Uncle Summerfield had married Thomas's sister, Eliza, at Gnosall
on October 8th 1829. Uncle James, Thomas's younger brother, had
married Ann Barlow at Gnosall on October 8th 1829. Double wedding!

17th February

Killed a small cow of Mr. P---y (Poyner)

A meeting about the tythe – The Association called

Lord Hatherton's Diary – Going to Cannock and Shareshill to get the Tithe Agreement signed.

Setled with Mr. Biddle

Received of Mrs. Dawe ?

Told Fanny Lovet to come on the 19th (see 10.2.40)

18th February

Mrs. R. Lindop called (sister-in-law, Hatherton)	1s 10d

Mrs. R Lindop- widow of Richard Lindop

S.G. called and broat 2 pigs puddings
S.G- wife of farmer James Gibbons?

Fanny came – called on Totty and was not home (22.4.40)

Mother went to Bloxwich

Bought 2 Heiffers of Mr. Corns
Mr. Corns- possibly John Corns, another Cannock butcher's was in Cannock in 1834.

Jane sent a couple of fowls for Mrs.?

Jane - Jane Walker, Thomas's sister in law and Mary's aunt.

20th February

Winnerd the Barley at Wyrley (very bad day- east wind frost & snow)
Fetched Calf from (Undjrs?)

21st February

Killed the Calf from Wyrley and 1 of Mr. P----sheep

Oyster night and give notice for the last

Another meeting of note was the Oyster Club. This was founded in Edinburgh during the late 18th Century and into the 19th century for the purpose of intelligent conversation. Anything could be discussed including art, architecture, philosophy, politics, science and economics. It was also a supper club eating dried salt haddock and oysters. The Lindop family were obviously part of this as subscriptions were made and the club was held at the Crown. They were regular subscribers to newspapers (*The Staffordshire Advertiser*?) and possessed and brought books, not common with the ordinary working man, so would be able to enter into intelligent debate. As this club was probably for men only, there was also a club for Ladies.

22nd February

Settled with Miss Gripton

Thomas Gripton was a farmer/ miller living in Walk Mill.

Paid Mr. Corns ? For 2 Heifers

Settled with Mr. Shute ? An error init

Received 3 black waistcoats of Mr. Biddle (aged 50,
Tailor & near neighbout

Uncle Joseph (Little Wyrley) called to see his calf, John Darby paid

Mary Lockley paid

Mary and William Lockley were tenants (house and garden) living in the row behind the Royal Oak. ᴬSee map. Son, John, was a bricklayer.

Father asked to Mr. Sants (lived in Mill Street)   1s 6d

Mr. Sant was an independent gentleman living in Cannock with 4 servants (3 female and one male).

Mill Street, Cannock where Mr. Sant lived.

23rd February

Paid Anslow for the Hedge at Huntington at 8/-d.

Per roof (see 24.3.40) – Sunday – so bitterly cold   10s 0d

    Thomas Anslow was an ag. labourer and a tenant living in Mill Street.

    (See map for plot 379)

24th February

Mary Askey paid 5.6d. Paid up tow day

    Mary Askey was a tenant. Elizabeth Askey, aged 45, also lived in

    Cannock.

Father went to tea at Mrs. Knight and supper and Mr. H---- was their.

S.E.L. went to Wyrley bought Mary a new frock and took it to

Marshall to be made

    Mrs.Knight was a lady of independent means who lived at 429 on the

    map, across from St. Luke's Church, in today's Mill Street. She lived

    there with daughter, Mary (45) and Ann Hudson (30) a female servant.

    Marshall was a hatmaker and millener and was possibly the sister

    to William Marshall, the druggist. In 1841 he was elected to be

    headborough of Cannock.

25th February

One of the Ewes lamb in the pen up the Garden   5s 6d

Sold Mr. N. Brookes some Barley – 40 bushels

    Nathaniel was a farmer of Norton. He died on 10-5-40 and his wife

    Mary continued to run the farm with her children.

25th February continued

Went to bleed a calf at Mrs. Walhouses

Saw Thos Lindop and thought him very ill

26th February

Went to Norton settled with Mr. Masfin

Bought 6 sheep and paid for them

Winerd the Barley

Sent that cow that came from Chatcull to Wyrley

27th February

Sent the Barley to Mr. N. Brookes to be made malt of 40 strike -
got the Oates in (see 18.3.40)

Herd that T. Lindop was worse of Hatherton (see 25.2.40)

Mr. R.H. called Mr. Oakley d-----

28th February

Killed one of Mr. Masfin sheep one of Mr. P----- and Mrs. Walhouse
calf.

Bout a grose of pipes to smoke with for J. Smith of Norton -
3/- for them

29th February

Weighed Mrs. Walhouse calf and one of Mr. P---- sheep,
one of Mr. Masfins by hand

Mother went to see Thomas Lindop (note – a leap year)

1st March

S.E.L. bonet sent from Bloxwich

R. Lindop dined at houre house

2nd March

Setled with Edwd. Smith

Cleaned 2 cow heels for Mrs. Walhouse

Bot beef of B---- for D----   ls 10d

William gon to wyrley took little Anslow with him (see 23.2.40)

Suthens? Came to Cannock (William Southerns Little Wyrley)
> Southerns is William an ag. labourer working for Joseph at
> Little Wyrley.

Weighed one of Wrights sheep

S.E.L. Gone to Wyrley

Paid E. Cope for newspaper for 1839
> E. Cope - William was a draper in Cannock in 1834. E. may be his son.

Market Place, Cannock.

Mr. Emmery called
> Mr. Emmery - Charles Emery was a bricklayer in Cannock.

Brot from Lichfield a copies of the Surrender of Mr. George Wade
and admittance thereof (see 18.9.1840 & 9.7.1840)   £1 1s 0d

2 Ewes lamed with one each

Killed one of Mr. Tomlinson sheep that a dog bit – a very good one
> Mr. George Tomlinson was a builder/farmer living down in the Longford
> Road area. Owned land there.

Fetched the Cheese from Chatcull 9 hundred and sixty pounds
(see 7.2.40)
   Uncle John of Chatcull.

Uncle John horse was very ill at Stafford After eight when
came home

Paid for Mr. Tomlins sheep

Had the back kitchen chimney swept

Went to Crown to the Oyster was to be the last

Fetched the sheep from Mr. Tomlinson

One of Mr. W----- sheep one of Mr. Masfins, one ewe lamed in
the yard and brot 2 lambs

Mary Lockley paid 5.0d. Towards her pig

S.E.L. Came from Wyrley (see 3.3.40)

Mary Ann Lindop and Eliz dine here today (sisters from L. Wyrley)

Mother went to Church in the morning

9th March

E.S.L.(Eliza) and Mary Ann (Lindop) went to see Mrs. Shorter
of Wyrley Bank
   Mrs. Mary Shorter aged 45 is the wife of William Shorter aged 45 from
   Cheslyn Hay. Wyrley Bank was the old name for it.

3 lambs came today

Mr. Price paid   £1 1s 0d
   William Price was a tenant living in Mill Street. He was a painter/glazier.

Setled with Cotton Acutt (account?)

Fetched Mrs. Knight coals 1. 5. 4d. Got them in the next day

11th March

Father went to Wolverhampton took the ten chicken

Had a new tap puton cost 3.6d.

Went to Hatherton after he came back for a calf and Mrs. Wal---
was going to kill it themselves

12th March

Bot and fetched Mr. Sheridan calf

Went to Wyrley

13th March

Setled with Mr. Cotton- the miller.

Received for wheat	£52 13s 5d
Mr. C. (Cotton?) Bill- probably from Pillarton Hall Farm.	£21 9s 1d

Paid Forrister
   Possibly William Forrester of Hednesford.

Paid J. Bamford

S.E.L. Went to Hatherton to bid Ann Farewell
   Probably Ann from Milton.

Bowling Green Cottage, Hatherton.

Settled with Mr. R. Bailey

Paid the Church Rate   7s 6½d

> Could be the stipend paid to the curate? Each churchgoer would be
> expected to pay a certain amount. Hence entry 28-2-40 Settled with
> J. Shiel in full.

14th March

J. Darby paid rent up today

**Setled with E. Biddle for mending the windows – the pains in
the back kitchen window 5d1/2 per pain**

> E.Biddle is son of William a tailor living in Cannock and is a painter and
> glazier.

Sent the hens to Wyrley and T. Lindop also went

15th March

Mr. Somerfield dined here today

**Mrs. Knight sent a large piece of fish and oysters (Sunday –
14 month of constant rain**

16th March

Killed a cow

Sold Mr. Wright a cow and calf

Hour newspaper

17th March

Sent the plants to Blox

Settled with Mr. W. Cope

> William Cope, a draper living in Cannock.

18th March

Father went to Wolverhampton

**Brewed four strike of malt that came on the 17 from being
make at Mr. N. Brookes – 10 bags came here and 4 went to
Wyrley – 40 bushel was sent to make malt off on the 27th Feb.
And came back on 17 March**

One of Mr. Wrights sheep today

Fetched coals from Forresters one load 2/3d. The other 10.7d1/4d/

Mrs. Wood called after takin old Mrs. W to Rugeley
Elizabeth Wood of Latherford House.

Worthington gin came today

Killed a little pig of own

Herd that Mother's Brother (J.Walker) **was leaving westwood**
(see 14.4.40)
> Does she mean Wetwood? That is where Joseph farmed before moving
> to Little Wyrley. There is NO Westwood in the Midlands! Joseph is
> obviously thinking of moving farms as he comes to Little Wyrley on
> 8-5-40 with his wife and Ann and Joseph had a cottage there.

S.E.L. went to see Mr. N. Brookes

Uncle Joseph called with his son Will was going to a sale
(William eldest son)

Mary Perrins paid up	5s 0d
Paid Mr. Poyner	£37 18s 0d

Mr. Wright fetched the cow and calf from Wyrley, herd that
Mr. Joseph Brinley of Walsal was dead

Settled with Shomaker Hall
Thomas Hall was a shoemaker and had been in Cannock in
1834. Lived in Mill Street. Ann Heath, a milliner, also lived with him.

Mrs. Dawson called

Grandmother went to Wyrley from Shareshill

Got F Jr? Lamb from Heaths

B---- Walsall for Mrs. Knight cost 10/6d.

Mr. Alsop called was cross that the box was not set
(20.1.40 and 23.2.40)

John Alsop was an ag. labourer in Cannock. Box was the type of hedge.

25th March

Fetched two load of thorns from Huntington

26th March

Sowed the peas at Mosswoods and Homes drill paid 5/0d.
For it same time

Mosswood was land in the Longford Road area which Thomas rented.
*See map.

28th March

Three sheep of Mr. N. Brookes

Mr. Tomlinson calf 110 at 6d1/2d   £1 19s7d

The calf of Mr. S. Wright

Paid for Poyners Peas which fetched   £1 3s 0d

Setled with J. Shiel in full

Paid Mr. T. Hall of Rumer Hill for Peas (see 6.4.40)
    Lord Hatherton's Diary – To Rumer Hill – Good luncheon there given by
    the Tenants. Hall a very good fellow, like his father before him (7.2.40)
    Thomas Hall was a 45 year old farmer at Rumer Hill, Leacroft. His wife
    was Hannah.

28th March

Mr. S. Selvester of Little Wyrley called and took tea with us
(see 3.4.40) and Mr. Sant (lived at Mill St.)

We have 34 lambs today

29th March

Father & Mother and 3 Brothers (Thomas, Richard, George)
went to see Grandmother and Ann at Mrs. H----

And Aunt Jane (Jane Walker) went and came back with us

Called at Mrs. Selvesters saw Mrs. Greensill and her baby

Thomas Greensill worked as an ag. labourer for Mary Walker at Little Wyrley.

Went to Norton about the tithe

Pinfold Farm, Watling Street, Norton Canes.

Setled in full with J. G. Stubbs

J.G Stubbs was an independent gentleman. He died on the 4-5-40 aged 45.

Mother spent the evening with Mrs. K---- (Knight)

Mr. Hill came up at 10'oclock to say that a ewe had a nother lamb she lamb one at 3 and the other between 9 and 10'oclock at night

31st March

John Sanders came to box the Garden at the barn (see 24.3.40)
John Sanders a gardener aged 50 living in Cannock.

31st March

Sowed the bed of carrots

William (Ward) fetched the coals from Mr. Gilpins   £1 0s 6d

1st April

Father went to Wolverhampton

2nd April

R.L. and G.L. Poorley – sister Jane went to Wyrley – Willington
calved – sowed the barley at Huntington

—HUNTINGTON.

3rd April

Sowed the Barley Sladland?

Settled with 3/0d. For loves Goodwin of Huntington (loves= loaves?)

Mr. Stubbs of Hammerwich called

Will cow calved (Willington)

Mr. Selvester of little Wyrley had a fire burnt all the Hay two hovels and cowshed, the cause – Emma Cliff twok hot ashes (----?)after backing (see 28.3.40)

4th April

Father took Grandmother to Stafford S.E.L. Went with them bought a new dress and a beautiful hiyacinth
> Grandmother is Mary Walker of Little Wyrley.

Killed 3 of Mr. N.B. sheep – a calf of Mr. Tomlinson and one that we had of Mr. Masfin

W. Lockley settled in full

5th April

Grandmother and T. Lindop from Hatherton diend with us

Rolled the barley Sladland (is a field in Mill Street *See map)

Settled with Mr. Prince
> George Prince, aged 20, was a clock/watchmaker in Cannock.
> Brother William, aged 25, was a cavalry officer.

6th April

Received of Mr. Stubbs of Hamerwich for 2 cowes   £26 13s 0d

Mr. T. Hall of Rumer Hill about sowing Barley to bye (28.3.40)

7th April

Jack came to say that a sheep could not lamb
> Jack- Jack Sylvester a labourer at Hatherton.

Mr. Price paid	£1 0s 0d

Ward (William) taken the Horses to Wyrley

Grandmother taken tea with Mrs.?

Father at Wyrley brot two sheep from Mr. N. Brookes	1s 4d

8th April

Ann Roberson left her place at Mrs. Browns Lichfield stopt 3 nights

Grandmother gone to Wyrley

Betty Darby paid for rent 5. 0d.

9th April

Emptying the pit in Cannock Croft *see map
    In Mill Street 374- could be Cess pits. Thomas owned that property and
    rented it out at 5s7d per annum.

Castrated the lambs – John Warbank did them one ewe bled a
teal to death

10th April

Killed 2 of Mr. N. Brookes sheep – one of Mr. Wright

Had half a pig of J. Lindop

Father went to Wyrley

Sowed the seeds in wrycroft and barn piece at the Hills
(Calving Hill?) – T. Butler sowed the celery

11th April

Salted the side of bacon

The heifer calved that we bought of Mr. Corns

Owen and Thomas are Executed, Ellis is respited was transported
    The Murder of Christina Collins (The Bloody Steps Murder) on the
    Trent & Mersey Canal at Rugeley. Christina Collins' body was found in
    the canal at Brindley Bank near Rugeley Aqueduct about a mile from
    the town at 5.0a.m. on Monday 17th June 1839. After a Coroner's
    Inquest at the Talbot Inn, Rugeley 3 boatmen, Owen, Thomas & Ellis,
    were charged with her murder & were committed to Stafford County
    Gaol. The trial was held at the Staffordshire Summer Assizes in July
    1839. Musson, the boy who was originally charged with them, was
    not named in the indictment. However the trial was put off until the

next Assizes on the grounds that a material witness, Mr. Joseph Orgill, a prisoner in the gaol, could not be heard until he had been granted a free pardon from the Secretary of State. It was understood that he had made (Owen) important disclosures to Orgill while in prison. At the second trial they were charged with wilful murder "by casting, pushing and throwing the said Christina Collins into the canal, by which means she was choked, suffocated and drowned".

Owen and Thomas were hanged in public at Stafford on 11th April, 1840. According to the newspaper reports, nearly ten thousand people were present to witness the macabre spectacle. They sat on walls, climbed trees, and even perched themselves on the roofs of nearby houses in order to obtain a good view. The hangman was William Calcraft. The commuted sentence of Ellis was that he should be transported for life to Australia. He returned initially to Stafford Gaol, where he became a changed character and his transportation was such that both the Prison Governor and the Chaplan wrote separate letters to the Visiting Magistrates and the result of this intervention was that the sentence was reduced from life to 14 years. At the trial he was judged to have been much less involved.

12th April

Beautiful rainey Sunday

The other heifer calved in the night that was bought of Mr. Corns

Walsall Road, Cannock.

13th April

Father Bought 4 lambs of Mr. Masfin

Gone to Lord Hatherton's sale and
bought a cow and brot home with him

IMPORTANT SALE OF PRIME FAT STOCK,
Belonging to the Right Hon. Lord Hatherton.
TO BE SOLD BY AUCTION,
BY MESSRS. LONG AND TAYLOR,
*At Teddesley Park Farm, on Monday, the 13th day of
April,* 1840,
THIRTY Short-horned COWS, seven Galloway
HEIFERS, three long-horned COWS, two
Scotch OXEN, one short-horned OX, one fat BULL,
120 fat WETHERS, eight fat CALVES, and fifteen
porket PIGS.
The sale to commence at eleven o'clock.

14th April

Killed it J. Warbank helped Uncle (beautiful day)

J. Walker came from Leek and went to Wyrley for is few goods
(20.3.40)
    (Mrs. Lindop's brother.)

Willingtons sheep in calvinin (Calving Hill?)
    Thomas rented land there. *See map.

Father gone to Wolverhampton

15th April

Brother stopt all night started at 5 this morning
    (Was this mother's brother, J. Walker? - See 14.4.40)

16th April

Received for fat Turner's (Cheslyn Hay)   £2 4s 11d

17th April

Good Friday – killed one of our lambs that was lamed
25th of February

Cream of Tartar on the stained spot, and twisting or tying that
part of the linen to keep it place,thus put it to boil –
no more trouble

Good Friday – killed one of Mr. Masfin lambs as well has
our own, one of Mrs. Walhouse calfs as well as one of
Mr. Sheridans, a large sheep that we had sometime of
Mr. Masfin

Setled with Haddocks

18th April

Mary Askey paid (beautiful day)   4s 0d

Our lamb was 27 lb. And so was Mr. Masfins – made on them both   £2 16s 2d

49

19th April

Mrs. J. & Mr. J. Lindop (Little Wyrley) and Mr. & Mrs. Gough came (not a cloud for over a fortnight, 10 days of hot sun)

S.E.L. and M.L. and R.L. and Father dined at Wyrley (Sunday)

Mrs. Knight sent us a large fish and took it to Wyrley

20th April

Father went to Walsall and S.E.L. went with him say Mr. R. Jesson and J. Walker went

21st April

Father went to Rugeley Fair (possibly the Horse Fair).

Elizabethan Cottages, in the Horse Fair, Rugeley

Paid Mr. Ward for Peas (Teddesley?)   £1 0s 0d

A Butcher cow drove to Hednesford pool and dropted J. Warbank fetched it and dressed in the Slaughterhouse and Mr. Buxtons horse and cart to fetch is. Davis of Willenhall paid 7.6d. for all trouble

Hednesford Pool existed on all old maps formerly comprised of 2 pools lying between the railway and Rugeley Road at Hednesford. Hednesford Lodge was built beside it in 1831. It covered about 27 acres in 1834 and was reduced to 23 acres in 1851.

J.Warbank- most likely to be John Wallbank of Hednesford, aged 50, who had a small farm at Pool End in Hednesford.

22nd April

Paid postman 7.9d. to take to Totty's (see 19.2.40) brought the
receipt the next day for land tax

23rd April

Killed one of Mr. Poyners sheep

Gave J. Bamford to give G. Webb ½ years Land Tax   14s 0d

24th April

Killed W. L. Gilpins calf – one sheep of Mr. Poyners and one pig of ours

25th April

Set the bishops potatoeas (see 7.2.40)

Paid Mr. Shutt for Leggins   1s 4d

William came from Wyrley

Sent 40 bushel of barley to Mr. N. Brookes

Stole 8 fowls and the Guinea-cock from Grandmothers

26th April

The first Sunday a sermon in the evening

27th April

**Mr. G. J. Stubbs died about 7.0.clock after a few days illness with
water in the chest (see 23.3.40) –**
  Gentleman George Stubbs was a fine well-built man, quite 6 foot in
  height who usually dressed in black clothes and lived where Lloyds
  Bank was in the 1890's.

Mr. Stubb's house on the left in Cannock.

28th April

Brewed 8 strike of malt

Killed one of our sheep

27th April

Bout a lage barrel of Mr. Cotton (Pillaton Hall?)   £1 10s 0d

Finished sowing Barley

29th April

Father gone to Wolverhampton

Bought a rearing calf

Gone to fetch the cows from Wyrley to go to penkridge Fair

Sold Mr. Masfin the 2 Heifers that he Bought of Mr. Corns

To cure bad eyes the Herb we use for (Warts?) and breast milk
to bath with

30th April

Took 2 cows to penkridge Fair and sold them

Tom and his Father, bought a fat cow at Mr. Cottons   £26 5s 6d

Sale pillaton Hall
> Mr. Cotton owns the Hall. Is this Mrs. and Miss
> Cotton who appear later in the diary?

Got the first reddishes out of the garden at
the barn

PILLATON HALL ANNUAL SALE.
PRIME FAT AND STORE STOCK,
The property of Mr. Cotton.
TO BE SOLD BY AUCTION,
BY MESSRS. LONG AND TAYLOR,
(Successors to the late Mr. J. Davison),
On the premises, at Pillaton Hall Farm Yard, on Thursday, the 30th day of April, 1840, being Penkridge
fair day,
TWENTY very prime FAT COWS.
Four excellent HEIFERS in-calf.
One Hundred and Thirty capital FAT WETHERS.
Two FAT CALVES.
A fine Black COLT, three years old, by *Bryn-y-Orkin.*
Grey COLT, two years old, by *Roderick.*
Also a six-inch wheel strong and convenient tilted
CART, equal to new, with iron box arms, very suitable
for a carrier's or miller's purposes.
☞ The Auctioneers with confidence recommend
the above superior property to the attention of their friends
and the public, and beg to assure them that the high
opinion always entertained of the Pillaton Stock will be
further confirmed by an inspection of the above.
✱✱✱ Sale to commence at twelve o'clock.

Pillaton Old Hall Penkridge

Killed a calf of Coopers of Norton – one of Mr. J. Lindop is to have half back – one of Mr. Masfins lambs 2 of our own

> Ann Cooper ran a farm there. No husband by 1841 Census. She had children (3 girls 2 boys) and 2 labourers, John Ingram aged 40 and his son Joseph aged 15.

Mr. Jeddwine called and tould us that he had taken an house for 5 years at Shifnell (see 19.1.40 &14.6.40)

Mr. G. J. Stubbs aged 44 years buried on 4th May (see 27.4.40)

2nd May

Herd that Mr. N. Brookes was very ill

3rd May

Father went to Wyrley and say the pretty heifers calf

4th May

And took Mr. G. Gilpins calf and paid
1.4.0d.

Jane Wa---- was at Latherford, I was to go but did not

> Jane was at Latherford, near Calf Heath in the Parish of Hatherton. The Woods live there.

Paid E. Marshall in full (see 14.12.40)

5th May

Mr. Price paid   £1 4s 0d

6th May

Took the colt to Hatherton that came from Chester

Oct. 3rd 1838 and left it for sheep

Killed one of Mr. Masfins lambs, and a calf that came from Wyrley

7th May

Association Dinner

> "The Cannock Association for the Prosecution of Felons" issued a notice to the affect that 15 guineas would be given to anyone who gave information leading to the apprehension and conviction of anyone who amused himself by committing highway robbery. 10 guineas was the fee for the information concerning law breakers, stealing hogs, sheep, cattle, etc. and for like information regarding

the stealing of geese and such birds, agricultural implements, etc. and for robbing orchards a reward of 2 guineas was paid. This notice was signed by a long list of names, including the surnames of Gilpin, Shenton, Thurston, Masfin, Collis, Wallhouse and Sant. An annual meeting of this body was held in the Crown Hotel on Thursday May 6th 1824.

Could this be one and the same?

This association elected town "police" to enforce it. In 1841 those officers were William Rogers, a cooper aged 28, as the town constable; William Marshall, the druggist aged 50, as headborough; and James Crackett, shoemaker aged 22 of Mill street, as the town pinner and crier.

Headborough- officer identical in function to a petty constable.
Pinner- officer one of whose duties was to impound stray animals.

8th May

Mothers boots paid   6s 0d

Sold Mr. W. Stubbs of Sharshill the sheep that came from H----

Uncle Joseph came to live in the cottage at Wyrley and his wife and Ann & Joseph Walker

Ann Walker and Joseph Walker - They first arrived in the area and lived in the cottage before they both bought farms in Little Wyrley next to each other. Previously Joseph had farmed in Wetwood.

Mrs. Wood called after spending the day at Mrs. Hig--- of rumer Hill

Killed the last sheep of Mr. Masfin

9th May

And the last lamb and one of our own

Mrs. G. Hawkes of Daughter (lived at Norton Hall)

George's wife. He was an independent gentleman living at Norton Hall.

The Hall, Norton Canes

10th May

Mr. N. Brookes died at half past 4 in the morning (see 2.5.40)

11th May

Ann Hall Daughter of the late Richard Hall buried – six ladies pull Bearers aged 18 had wite scarfs and Hoods, silk
> On Sunday last (May 9th) at Cannock aged 18, Ann, only surviving daughter of the late Mr.Richard Hall of Shenstone. Hall deeply regretted by all who knew her.

Father gone to fetch a cow from Pillaton and Brother T with him

PILLATON OLD HALL

R.W.B. Collis came to look at it (Vicar)
> Rev. W. B. Collis was remembered for his deep toned voice and as a sportsman who carried more than one fowling piece. He was also issued with a Game Certificate at a cost of £4.0.10d each; others were Francis Hill of Cannock, Robert Masfen of Norton Canes and Wyrley, Michael Walker and Nathaniel Worsey of Cannock.

12th May

Paid Mr. Prince Land Tax for Essington   3s 6d

Killed it the cow – J. Warbank gone to fetch the two two yearholds from Wyrley to take to ley?

Mr. Poyner and Father took them the number 42 on the horn

13th May

Took Beef for Mr. N. Brookes funeral (see 10.5.40)

14th May

Uncle Walker and Uncle J. Lindop gone to Stafford Fair

Bought an horose? (Horse?) of the railway people   8d

15th May

Bought a pair of scizzers of S. Clowlow – received a note from
Mrs. Wood for Jane to go to keep house wile she went out

(Barthso?) called and (Stays?) in a month   12s 0d

16th May

Mrs. Askey paid   5s 0d

Setled S. Smith for mending   3s 6d

William went to Wyrley

G. Mother went to Mrs. Woods (see 15.5.40)

17th May

Sunday herd that T. Hill died after eating a very harty supper of
hot bread – Mrs. Knight very much hurt and his going to berry him
– cost 5.1.0d. besides the coffin
   T. Hill- Thomas Hill who lived at Rumer Hill.

20th May

Father went to (Mr. Bussells?) sale bought nothing

21st May

A young man called from Mr. Brights and paid for the beef
(Lord Hatherton's bailiff?)

George took ill of the measles

Took a Calf from Mr. Jenneys (farmer at Norton) to Wyrley

22nd May

Brough another back and killed it and one from Hatherton
Mrs. Walhouses

Paid Mrs. Hand's rent
   Mother of Thomas's first wife. Thomas rented a field from her at Longford
   Road area at 4/9d per annum. Part of Rogan's Meadow. *See map.

Sowed on the 20th soot on the Barley at carvonshill a cart
boddy full on the small field belos were the foot road goeas

Paid Joseph Weeb for howing the peas at the Mosswoods	£1 5s 0d

23rd May

Mr. Jenney had a dispute over 22lb. Of Veal that was bout on the
2nd May – paid him for his calfs, one living on the cow at Wyrley
(see 21.5.40)

Little Cope died
    Buried at St.Luke's.

Sent the sow and pigs to Wyrley, lent J. Walker the main, to go
tow Newport

24th May

Sunday R.W.B. Collis preached

W. Collis called

Grandmother hear

25th May

Went home with Thomas as he went to thrash

Mrs. Knight coals	£1 1s 10d

26th May

Paid J. Benton (Carpenter living in Cannock aged 25) for Ironing to squitch Rakes	2s 0d
Paid J. Bamford for mending the harnesh	8d

Cleaned ditto

Received 6lb. Of turnip seed from J. Lindops of Hatherton

27th May

Father went to Wolverhampton – saw Mr. Lea – he told him that
if Mr. Walkers meaning Mothers Family were the longest livers
wehen he died they should have is propity if he had any when
he died

28th May

Sowed the turnips in the hill peace Sladlands

29th May

Fineshed in ditto

Killed 2 of Mr. Poyners sheep – one of Mr. Tomlinsons calfs ditto lambs, in the week one of our own

30th May

Grandmother came to-day – paid the weed hers off at 10d.
Per day and one quart of bear

31st May

Mother and Father and S.E.L. went to Hammerwich –
saw his 20 fat cows for sale

1st June

Had Harthers cow in the weat promise to pay the damage
(see 1.7.40 &1841 Census page 21

Father bot 5 sheep at the sale

2nd June

Brewed 3 strike of Malt

4th June

Began to sow the blake field turnips

5th June

Killed 2 of Stubbs sheep – 2 of Mr. Tomlinsons

Lambs one on the 3 and one now

Jack Darby paid   5s 0d

Bot Mother a pair of shoes of the Still Man from Stafford –
Father paid for them   3s 0d

S.E.L. had 6.6d.

6th June

Bought 9 sheep of Mr. Masfin from Rugeley Fair and killed one
Rugeley Horse Fair- business was "flat". The attendance from London
and country dealers was poor. First class horses not numerous, the
best belonging to Joseph Boulton of Castle Church and Mr.Mann of
Marston Hill near to this town.

Jack Darby paid   2s 0d

7th June

R.W.B.Collis preached

8th June

Had 12 Crreys? From Wyrley for Gorge

Father went to Walsall

Paid W. Harrison (mine owner)
   (*In miners book page 168) possibly for Lime.

9th June

Paid Strongitharm	£4 4s 0d
Cooper to Decr 1829	£6 14s 0d

10th June

Went to Wolverhampton

Father had the sheep – fineshed sheering and lambs

Paid Mr. Masfin for his sheep that was bot at Rugeley Fair
on the 3 of June

11th June

Gave Mr. Masfin and (Mr. Harry?) towards the fresh Clergy set
is name down   10s 0d

Not gave are to have it

Father went to Hatherton and bot. Some lambs of J. Lindop –
came back and killed one lamb and sheep after

12th June

Killed two sheep and one lamb

13th June

Finessed sowing the brickel turnips

Put the wool up 37 fleeces

Received of Mr. Price   £1 0s 0d

Rich Lindop called from H----- was

14th June

All went to church besides Mother and me, Mary (15) received one pound of bride cake from R.W. Jendwin (see 1.5.40)

Sketch of St. Luke's Church with Poyner's house next door c.1840.

16th June

Paid Mr. Rogers for a dolly head   1s 0d

Had the thresh-amachine at Wyrley – it was went/weat that growed blake field

17th June

All tiered from the dust

18th June

Killed a lamb that came from Hatherton – Mrs. Lindops

19th June

Killed one sheep from (D.V.?) 2 more and one lamb

Went to Mr N B sale

20th June

Betty Darby paid

Elizabeth Darby, aged 50, lived in Mill Street. Tenant.   2s 0d

Father went again to Mr. N. Brookes sale and S.E.L. and T.L. with him – bot a great many things(see 10/13/5/40

21st June

Sunday M.L. gone to play with Miss carlet at Mr. Cottons
> Miss Carlet- Mary Scarlett's daughter who lived at Cotton's mill,
> possibly after father's death(27-5-41).

22nd June

Began to Mow the seeds at Wyrley

23rd June

T. Goodman (Ag. labourer who lived at Hednesford, aged 70)
came on Monday and today and Wensday to how turnips

24th June

Maid a Cherry pye for the Club

Killed 3 of Mr. Poyners lambs

25th June

A little showers for the club, kept no club

Mr. Shorter called has he came back from Stafford- was very hod

**Mrs. Witehed died in the Church yard, came in well and died in
one Minet**
> Mrs. Whitehead- wife of William. He was an
> ag. labourer living at Hawkes Green. He died aged 72.

26th June

S.E.L. and G.L. & M.L. R.L. gone with sister to Wyrley

Master gone to dine at Mr. Withnalls (Royal Oak)(there in 1834)

27th June

Mrs. Askey paid	**4s 0d**
John Darby paid	
Son of Elizabeth Darby	**1s 6d**
S.E.L. came back from Wyrley (see 26.6.40)	

28th June

**Father send Thomas L to take Grandmother to Church –
herd that Mrs. Mi Walker was left Cannock**

29th June

Mowing the seeds at carvenshill

30th June

Sold Mr. Cotton 30 bags of weat that groed in the blake field
9.8d. per strike

Loadinded two load of seeds at Wyrley

Paid Loyon? Of Penkridge for one strike of Rygrass   7s 6d

New sack   2s 3d

The right time to sow Cabbage seed the 5th August

1st July

Henry Arthur died (see 1.6.40)
 Henry Bailey Arthur, jockey. He was only 21 when he died, buried on
 6-7-40. Son of Henry Arthur, horse trainer/farmer, who lived along
 Hednesford Road near today's Stoney Lea Road.
 *More on both in Hednesford Horse Racing History by Anthony Hunt.

2nd July

John Chamberlin buried

Mr. Price paid   £1 0s 0d

Settled with Mr. S. Selvester on the late Mr. N. Brookes account

3rd July

Killed 2 of the lambs that came from Hatherton and one sheep out
of the field

R.L. came from Hatherton after we was in bead

4th July

Gave him for to take Mr. J. Lindop towards the cheese – he was
unwell that he Could not come,   £20 0s 0d

Sowed the wite fringue on the bed in the fur room

Bottled some brandy and Gin

Carried the seeds at Wyrley

Mary boots paid   5s 0d

5th July

Went to Hatherton and drank tea – Mother and S.E.L. and G.L.
Mrs. Walker was there

6th June

Settled with Mr. Leadbeater in full, talking about Mad Dogs
(see Hatherton Diary 5.7.40

    James Leadbeater, aged 55 - farmer from Old Fallow area.

For the Oyster club   14s 4$^{1}/_{2}$d

Mrs. Wood came and brot some cherries

7th July

Mrs. Byrch of Huntington paid – said would bring the other soon   10s 0d

    Probably Hannah Byrch.

R.L. of H dined with us (Richard Lindop of Hatherton)

8th July

Carried some of the seeds

9th July

Showers, Keeper Wade Married (see 4.3.40)

10th July

Fetch the lambs from Hatherton, had half a calf of corns

Killed one lamb that came from H--- one of our own and the
last sheep of Mr. Masfins

11th July

Fineshed carrieng the seeds at carvanhill

Mr. William of the Old Hall called and R.L. from H

12th July

Had a fresh clergyman

13th July

Gone to Mow the Grass at the Stonall
meddow

Had a pain put in the window in the
room over the – paid for it
3d.

One in the back kitchen – paid for it
5d.

14th July

Killed one of our own sheep

15th July

St. Swithins, very hot and drying, washed and dryed, and mangled
and aired a coverlid in 3 hours

Carried 3 load of hay from the Stonnall meadow

16th July

Rains

17th July

Fineshed carrieng the Stonnall medow

Mrs. Walhouse called and Mr. Mac--- (Macdurmot – see 9.2.41)
wishing to take lodgings
    John Macdurmot, aged 25, curate of the parish.

Weighted the Wool

Sent Polly to fetch her Father was but two hours away

Fanney Lovet and S.E.L. gone to Wyrley haymaking

18th July

J. Warbank making is own hay

S.E.L.came back (overnight stay?)

19th July

Sunday had Mrs. Lindops pork for dinner – 31/2 lb

20th July

Pays rent at the street road

Old Mrs. Hawkes called the first time after her Illness
(mother-in-law of Mrs. G. Hawkes ?)
    Charlotte Hawkes aged 70, living at Norton Hall. Independent lady
    and mother-in-law to Mrs. G . Hawkes.

21st July

Bot a pair of side come of the Irishman for S.E.L.   2s 9d

Brewed 3 strike of Malt – gave 1.0d. per lb. For hops

T.W.L. wet to take Grandmother to Walsall

Black cherrys were 3 pence per lb.

22nd July

Father went to Wolverhampton T.W.L. with him and J. Warbank
as well

Bot a fat cow and a calf to feed one (on?)a cow and 4 lb.
Of cherries for 11d.

23rd July

Paid Mr. Thacker for one years (Leves?) for Little Wyrley   £1 5s 11d
    John Thacker aged 65, farmer at Norton under Cannock.

Richard taken poorly – killed one of our lambs

24th July

Killed the large calf that was fed one (on?) the Chatcull cow

Mrs. & Miss Weeb of Haywood drank tea here

Mr. Homes (doctor)came to see Richard   £1 5s 6d
    Thomas Homes, aged 30 a surgeon at Cannock. He lived next door to
    Mrs.Knight in Mill Street.

25th July

Paid J. Warbank

Paid Mr. (Crosser/Croper?) Norton for calf   £1 11s 0d
    Mr. Cooper, farmer at Norton. He had died by the 1841 census and
    his wife Ann was keeping the farm.

Killed Calf as had been on a Cow at Hills and ?   £5 5s 0d

Fetched a load of coal from Mr. Foresters load   8s 4d

Grandmother come to see Richard and found him Ill (see 23.7.40)

26th July

Aunt Jane was her (here?)

27th July

Forrester coals   7s 7d

Paid Mr. S. Sylvester to the late Mr. N. Brookes (see 20.6.40)

For Mrs. Knight for Malt   £3 16s 0d

Fineshed carrying the hay at the Hills

28th July

Mowed the Brickell Meddows

Jimey the Irishman came bot Father a bottle of Wiskey

Killed one of Mr. Wrights sheep

29th July

Weighed 59 lb. Bot of Mr. Tomlinson sheep and lambs	£8 5s 0d
J. Darbey paid	6s 0d

30th July

Bot a pig of J. Warbank	13s 0d

Mrs. Fargissn (?) children very noughty
> Mrs. Fargusson, wife of Daniel Fargusson, ag. labourer living in Mill
> Street. He died on 23-4-48. Children were James (10); John (7);
> Emma (5); and Joseph (3). One other son, William (15) was working
> for John Barley a baker aged 25 in Cannock.

Herd that Mr. Stubbs was hert

31st July

Killed the cow that bot at Wolverhampton very good one

Finished the Hay – had five wagon load at the brickel

1st August

Took the Beef to Norton

2nd August

Paid J. Lindop of Har---- for lambs	£12 5s 0d

Children gone to get bilberrys

Mary diend with Miss Carlet (see 21.6.40)
> Could be Catherine the 9 year old daughter of Mary the wife of
> Mr. Scarlett, doctor. By the 1841 census the baby, Elizabeth, was 9
> months old.

3rd August

S.E.L. drank tea with Mrs. K and Miss R of B Mrs. And
Miss Cotton (Pillaton Hall?)

4th August

Mrs. Walhouse would not have it back (loyn?) of Beef Because we we had to by it from a town

Mr. Price paid   £1 1s 0d

5th August

Went to Wyrley – saw that J. Smith had cut is hay rick and it was very black

> James Smith- farmer aged 35. Mother was Dorothy aged 70 and he had a brother, William aged 40.

Came back by great wyrley and called at Mr. Shorters and the Mrs. Had a bad leg

> Mrs. Shorter- Mary Shorter aged 45.

Went to Hatherton and bot a cow and calf   £10 17s 6d

Grandmother came with him

Bot S.E.L. Gloves 3

6th August

The ladys Club bot a little cloase horse (at door?)   1s 6d

7th August

Grandmother went to the Mosswoods and got a strike of Peas

8th August

Calf 124 sheep 73

Mr. Wrights paid Mr. Smith of sum for shoes   11s 2d

> Mr. Samuel Smith was a shoemaker in Cannock. He was there in 1834. Mr. Wright is probably Wright of Wolverhampton.

S.E.L. and her Mother and Father started to go tow Chatcull with the Chestnut Mare when they got past Radford bridge her fell and cut both her knees so very bad that they returned hom with Thankfulness, Aunt Jane was here to take care of home

Mowed the Barley in the Sladlands

Chatcull old farm.

9th August

Young Addams that his at Somervills died

Mr. Byrch and Mr. Jemey and Elen James gave us some gooseberries

10th August

Mrs. Askey paid owes 2.6d.	5s 0d

Mr. J. Wright of Wolverhampton sent is cousin J. Phillip Wright for
S.E.L. to take her to the races, but her Father did not wish her to go
  Wolverhampton Races which were always held in August on Mon/
  Tues/Wed of the week around the 10th. Those race meetings began
  in 1825 when the course was built.

Brot Gig Mothers Shoes new	3s 3d
Aunts	4s 6d

11th August

Father ver cross about Mars nees (see 8.8.40)

12th August

Washed 3 Blankets

Mr. & Mrs. Somerfeild called to ask us to the wake
  Eliza, Thomas's sister, and William. The Wake is presumably Cannock
  Wake.

Mrs. Jenney and Mrs. Hall called

Mrs. Elizabeth Jenney aged 70 of Norton and Mrs. Hannah Hall aged
40 of Leacroft.

Mr. Wright sent T.L. new cloths

13th August

Began to Mow the Oates

Fineshed badgering the peas at Mosswoods

Paid Mr. Thomas (local blacksmith) **for Ellrake**   10s 0d

Killed 2 lambs and one sheep

14th August

Norton races

**I bought a nail brush and a tooth brush & a brush to clean tooths
(comely?)**   1s 8d

Mr. J. L. Was at the races very tipsy (John Lindop of Hatherton)

15th August

Mr. Wrights sheep 65 lb.

Grandmother went to hammerwich found Mr. Stubbs very poorly

Bot a brest of veal of J. War and paid for it

16th August

**Bloxwich wake (see 12.8.40) F. & M went — Uncle Joseph Walker
there Ellen Barlow and Miss Williams called**

Ellen Barlow was sister to Ann Barlow married to James.
Miss Williams daughter to Mr. Williams of Old Hall near Pillaton.

17th August

S.E.L. gone to Blox Races

These Races, which are always held on the Wake, Monday and
Tuesday as reported in the *Wolverhampton Chronicle*.

Mr. Curtis called and Father went with him to Calving Hill

Bot 2 sickels   1s 6d

18th August

Bewed 4 Strike of Malt, had the hops
of Mr. Turner gave 16 per -----?

19th August

Bot a pieces of Organ Meadow and other Land in Mr. Tomlinsons
occupation of Mr. James Tibbitts solicitor, Warwick, the morning
after sale

Organ Meadow was in the Longford area- owned by Thomas.

*See map.

20th August

S.E.L. came home an Grandmother

Paid Mr. Wright   £13 12s 0d

Paid Mr. Harvison for roads   £1 13s 11d

21st August

Carried the Sladlands Barley all but one load

22nd August

Betty Darby paid   1s 6d

23rd August

Mother & Father & S.E.L. went to Hather--- wake ther was four
Mrs. Lindops together

Thomas's wife Mary; Mary Lindop of Hatherton; Elizabeth Lindop,
Joseph's wife, and possibly James's wife.

24th August

Fair bot Mr. J. Poyners sheep 23 at 1.3.0 each

Bot 2 heifers of T. Darby that he bot at Wolverhampton Fair(17.2.0d.?) back

Mr. Chamberlin paid for Chris beef

Fineshed the Sladlands Barley, and 2 load of Oates from the Brickel

25th August

Fineshed the Oates and one load of peas upon them

26th August

Gone to Huntington for the Barley – Sut & But gon a mowing to Wyrley – put 2 load of peas on the Barley

27th August

Fetched 11 load of peas, fineshed the field, F. Balam helped, W. Sothern sketched the wall at the Barn on the left side, and sent it all down and the door as well, thanks be to God that no one was hert

28th August

Top the ricks up – rained at night

Mrs. Rogers had a son
Wife of John Rogers a bricklayer aged 30 of Cannock. They named him William.

29th August

Paid the Irishman for Mosswood	£1 5s 3d

Gone to carri wheat at the Hills

30th August

Brot a couple of ducks with them from Wyrley

Sunday Grandmother is her went to Church twice

31st August

G. went to Wyrley

1st September

Father went to Wolverhampton back by ¼ to 11 o'clock

Washed one blanket – rained in the afternoon

2nd September

Mr. Holland sent a brace of birds – rained here and not at Wyrley –
carried the Barley at the back at the Barn at Hills

3rd September

Carried at night 4 load of Moss woods weat

4th September

Fineshed the weat and carried the Barley at the Stonameddow
the middle (Which Thomas rented) had

5th September

Large wagon load

Betty Darby paid	1s 6d

Fanney Lovet went to penkridge to be Confermed went at one and
came back after 9 o'clock – behaved her self very Ill a bout her work

6th September

Sunday – Mother went to see Mrs. Brinley – found her very Ill
(see 14/18/22.9.40)

7th September

Mrs. Knight sent a large peace of Fish

Mr. Price paid	£1 0s 0d

Carried the Barley at calvinghill that the soot was sow upon
4 loads of Barley

8th September

Bot George a new pair of Boots out of the Market   2s 9d

Bot a large meat dish   8d

Washed 2 Blankets

Carried the weat lower calving hill

9th September

Fineshed harvest – carried the weat at Hills and roy croft

10th September

Mrs. Knight coals from Brown Hills – got them in the same night   £1 2s 3d

11th September

J. Warbank was to come and did not

Bot ¼ of greengaues 8 to preserve

Mr. Hill gave us a dog welp of a favourite spannel of G. J. Stubbs
our helpa

12th September

Add Pork one of our own very nice add

The Harvest Supper

13th September

Grandmother and Mother drank tea at Mrs. Knights – she read a
letter from Mrs. Green and she was Traviling in wales, and saw the
bust of Stephen and Maud

14th September

Grandmother went to see Mrs. Brinley for the last time

15th September

Father went to Lord Bradfords and bot a cow and brot it home T.L.
was with him

16th September

Killed it and took G. To Wyrley

17th September

Sold it and Mr. P---- called at night

18th September

Went with whale Mrs. Walhouse keeper to kill some game for
Mrs. Knight – only found 3 birds and one hare – took them over
that night – was pleased with them (see 4.3.1840) whale could be
Wade (see 9.7.1840)

Killed the bees at Wyrley – one stung Aunts lip

The book man called

Mrs or Miss? Knight gone to Birmingham – aunt Jane come to keep
Mrs. K company – Mr. K. Fetched them

Mrs. Brinley died Sept 17 aged 68 years (see 14.9.40)
 Mary Brindley who was buried on the 22nd September.

19th September

Grandmother sent a large cock fowle from Wyrley

20th September

Me & Mother went to Shareshill say Mrs. Daw baby – drank tea
at Mrs. Woods (of Latherford).

21st September	
Bot 11 custard glasses	7s 0d
A slop bucket at Mrs. Halls sale	5s 0d

22nd September

Mrs. Brinley Buried

Walsall fair – Onion's (3?) rive?

23rd September

Thomas Anslow thatched the large wheat rick and put his knive in
the rick and lost it

24th September

Mrs. K. As got a dredful cold

Emted the yard of manure to te Moss wood pea stuble

25th September	
Fetched coal from the mill	5s 2d

J. Warbank here today the only one this week

26th September	
Father & Richard gone to Wyrley	
Mr. Price paid	£1 0s 0d

27th September

Sunday Mr. Selvester drank tea hear

28th September

Began to sowe weat in the Moss woods

28th September

Had the chimney swept paid 6 and a peice of bread and cheese

29th September

Had the shop acid pantry wite washed and the back kitchen and
the passage upstairs

Father took Mrs. Hawks Letters to Norton and brot them back

Miss Knight returned from Birmingham (see 18.9.40)

Fineshed the breauhouse

Fineshed the Moss woods

1st October

Mr. Somervill paid is bill

Aboretum at Derby opened on Wednesday the last day of Sept
1840. It comprises an Area of eleven acres of land is laid down
in spacious gravel walks extending more than six thousand feet
which are 15 feet wide seats are placed convenient situations, the
Ground arranged and planted in the most tasteful style of Modern
landscape affording elegant slopes planted to the best advantage,
a kind of zone has been formed of thousands of evergreens,
numerous forests trees and deciduous shrubs the free gift of Mr.
J. Strutt and a correct likeness of Mr. Strutt exhibited with this
Motto – Look here, we shall never see his like again

2nd October

Jon Darby	5s 0d

3rd October

Paid Mr. Smith for shoes	9s 2d

2nd October

Fetched coals from Brownhills	7s 0d

Killed the calf that came from Hatherton 36lbs. Per quarter

William Ward hert T.L. sheep leg brok it in trying to pass

Mrs. J. Walker and Uncle went to Banger

4th October

Mr. J. Lindop diend at hour house and Mr. Selvester aunt Jane
came to Mrs.(B.C/L?)

5th October

Brewed 4 strike of Malt

Mr. Cotton paid for the weat

Paid Mr. Corns for Beef	£2 3s 0d

Fetched the two heifers out of the Lea paid   £4 0s 0d

Mrs. Hill (Rumer hill) called about a calf

Mr. J. Lindop called had bot some bacon at Jennings

Mr. Masfin sent a Goose

7th October

Masons building at the Barn

Bot a little Poney

8th October

Paid Mr. Poyner for sheep   £39 4s 0d

Bot of Mr. Tomlinson sheep

9th October

Fetched (---?) (dt?)

10th October

Father fetched two cows from Witegrive – T.L. went with him

Bot a Goose of Uncle J. Walker – aunt came with him from
Stafford – went frome here after 7'oclock

Paid for the Goose   5s 0d

Miss Knight called to give Father for the sermons   £1 0s 0d

Paid Mr. Smith for noseing Thomas shoes   6s ½d

I bought a frock of Mrs. Byrch ? come to   8s 8d
     Mrs. Birch wife of Edward a shoemaker in Cannock?

Father and Thomas went to Stafford for the two cows

11th October

J. Darby paid   1s 6d

Father & Mother and S.E.L. went to Norton Church –
they Gatherd   £9 9s 6d

12th October

Killed one of the Cows that came from Witgrive

13th October

Began to get potatoes up

Received of Mrs. Dawe   £7 7s 0d

Herd that Mrs. Woodward was dead – Mary Hall that was

14th October

S.E.L. and Father went to Wolverhampton and bought a Bottle of
Port and Sherry Wine – each   3s 9d

Defreat (?) Raisins 71/2 lb – Volatile Salts 1.1/2 an oz

Cotton for (scarf)?

10 Gallon Saucepan   3s 6d

Poker   2s 0d

(Hiarc?) Shovel   3s 0d

Paid for plough   17s 0d

Mr. Burton/Buxton? Paid for bacon	£3 11s 6d
Bot George a pair of Boots	3s 6d

15th October

T.L. went to the barn to put the sheep in the seeds and found
one dressed? In the barn

16th October

Paid Mr. Tomlinson for sheep 7 at 1.6.0d.	£9 2s 0d
Bot 3 lambs but not paid for them at 18 each – at the same time one ewe sheep	£1 5s 0d
Went to Heartherton and bot of J. Lindop 20 sheep at	£1 14s 6d
And at the same time one of W. Lindop	

18th October

John Darby paid	1s 6d

19th October

Paid J. Webb land tax	14s 0d
Mr. Flintoff paid to Beef	£1 1s 6d
(Horse trainer living at Prospect House, Hednesford)	
Sold J. Lindop an heifer	£12 0s 0d
Paid Mr. Hobbey(?) for malt – in January 22	£1 10s 0d
Paid Mrs. Knights at the same time bot October 5	£1 18s 0d
Sold R. Lindop of Norton the first meat today	
Mr. Jenney sent the half sovereign as he borrowed	
Mrs. Knight paid Henneys Bill for ridge tiles	10s 0d

20th October

Killed the goose that Father bot J.W. at Stafford (see 10.10.40)

21st October

J. Wal and S.E.L. went to latherford (see 4.5.40)

Father received a coppy of the Title for the Land that he bot
(see 19.8.40)

22nd October

Killed a cow that came from Whitgreave

Mr. Sant brot us an hare – made the puddings and boiled the 12 hours

23rd October

Killed a small cow that came from Mr. Cottons

Mrs. G. Went to Latherford and came back with S.E.L. and J.W.
(see 4.5.40, 14.12.40, 21.10.40)
  Latherford, Staffs- a very small hamlet with just 2 houses.

24th October

Cut up the wake beef

Mrs. Knight sent a very large Fish by Father Lewice

Began the barn boors (doors?)

Father took the Beef to Norton in the afternoon

Killed 4 fowls

Herd that Gorge batty was dead – ad been delirious for a fortnight

J. Birch of Huntington paid towards potatoes   £1 0s 0d

Setled with J. Warbank   £2 2s 0d

25th October

Ther was 3 strangers to dinner, was very happy

26th October

Had a very good supper

27th October

Hednesford races W. Stubbs (See Racing Book by Anthony Hunt)

28th October

J. Darby paid   1s 6d

? called from Tedlesy – Mrs. Walhouse sent an hair

Had Mr. Masfins drill to sow weat at calvsinghill –
left at 12.0'clock, came at ¼ before 7.0'clock

S.E.L. and M.L. and J. Walker went to take tea at Mrs. Knights,
Mrs. Lindop of Little Wyrley sent some books

29th October

J. Lindop (James or Joseph as they were Ann's brothers) **from Milton
called was going to fetch Ann from Penckridge –** she came by the
"rale rode" (see 2.12.40) – (Cutting edge technology at the time – the
railway - the station at the Spread Eagle. In Lord Hatherton's Diary of
1.2.40 "By the railroad to Teddesley, reached Penkridge (from London) in
6 hours having set down by a first class train, Lord Stanley & many other
Members on the train. Travelling by stage coach would have taken 17
hours on the same journey."

The sow piged, brot 9 but 2 only lived – thout her tow fat, had
one in a basket – it died next day

30th October

Father been at Lichfield with Uncle Joseph

J. Warbank here the first day since settled

31st October

Saturday paid Mr. Poyner for tax land as well`   £1 5s 6d

J. Wbk here today

Mrs. Walker called had tea – Sunday (the first)

2nd November

Load Coals Brownhills   7s 10d

3rd November

Cut 30 of the Lambs hears

Uncle Joseph called and talked about the Shares of the Stubbses

Uncle James (Thomas's younger brother) **called was going
to Chatcull**

Marked the sheep that came from Hatherton

The balloon passed through yesterday – droped not far from the crosses – had a chase and went in it – came from wesbromage

Gorge had H & T Cope and Charles Stubbs for 2 hours
(Young friends.)

Four Crosses, Hatherton.

4th November

Uncle James came back from Chatcull, it was the court received a letter from Mr. Tibbets of Warwick (solicitor see 19.8.40) – and Lady Kenidy called
(Could be Mr. Kennedy the schoolmaster's wife?)

5th November

Had Mr. Buxton (Joseph Buxton aged 55 a saddler) and Josepeh Withnall

Uncle Joseph and J. Smith called

Bot a horse Mr. Thackera gave £17 at 5.0d. for it

6th November

J. Warbank was here today

Mrs. Wood and Ann Williams went to see Grandmother

7th November

J. Warbank was here – Mrs. Byrch paid

8th November

Gradmother came her for dinner

Mr. Selvester went to look at a Colt and J. Lindop with them

9th November

Killed a cow that came from Mr. Tomlinson

Went to Penkridge for a bondsman for R. Lindop

10th November

Went to Walsall say Mr. Curtis

Bot a turkey for Mrs. Knight gave   4s 3d

Mr. Goodwin called about the coult

Father bot it said it was foeled in May   £21 12s 6d

J.W. half a day hall day yesterday

12 A pair new and Irons   2s 7d

11th November

Sowing weat at the commin peace with weat

Mrs. Knight has a very bad cold — Mother went and supt with her

W. Sothers ground 9 strikes of Malt

12th November

Father went to Rugeley

Bot 35 lb of Hops 1/6d per lb and 6 lb of candles	3s 3d
Sold potoeas of the common peace for	£7 10s 9d

13th November

Brewed 9 strike of malt — a very hevy rainey day, fiensed sowing
the common piece

14th November

J. Darby	1s 6d

J.W. half a day yesterday

On the 10 Father bot a turkey for Mrs. Kt at Walsall for 4.3d.

Mrs. Lindop sent a book by Father Florence Graham

15th November

Mothers Brother called had seen Mr. Lewece had 35 fat cows tied up

16th November

The taken Gravel from the hojuse that Miss Wrights (The Miss
Wrights ran a Dame school in Cannock in 1834) used to keep school in
young parkes (Son of Rebecca Parkes an independent lady living in the Old
Fallow area) has bot and going to make two of it

Father brot the Colt from Mr. Shimnel of the yew tree house

Paid J. Goodwin in the presentence of Mr. Shimel — gave the 26/-d. Back out of the other	£21 10s 0d

17th November

Mrs. R. Lindop and Mrs. Hart spent half a day with us, Mr. Miller
showed is box — got half a rick of old Barley in that of growed at
calvinghill

18th November

Mr. Price paid	£1 0s 0d

19th November

Fetched the pig from Hatherton & killed it

Fetched Mrs. Knights Coal – Ward & Sutherns got them in

Took the colt and poney Wyrley

20th November

Bot a cow of Mr. Poyner to feed   £12 0s 0sd

21st November

Mrs. J. Lindop came and stop all night

23rd November

Mary Askey paid   3s 0d

22nd November

Was Sunday had Mrs. J. And Mrs. J. Lindop and J. Lindop
stopd dinner

23rd November

Father saw the Colts at the Hills
    (Hednesford Hills where they trained.)

F.B. sent to prison
    He was 19 years old and his trial was 29th June 1841.

24th November

Sent Fat by Clark have 4 cows up a feeding have had them above
a week

25th November

Ann Walker called brot a letter to go to the post, Father tould her
she ought to come before
    Ann Walker the daughter of John Walker a farmer at Little Wyrley.

26th November

S.E.L. and R.L. and Mother went to gayley was 4.1/2 hours away,
was rags birned drawing turnips from the br---el?

27th November

Father going to Wyrley

Killed Mr. Wrights calf

28th November

Weight 112 lb.

Betty Darby paid   1s 6d

Little Smith (son of landlord at Fleur de Lys) died at the fleur-de-lis –
J. Warbank said he had been 9.1/2 days and 2 days this week

29th November

Sunday T. Lindop of H diend her, they sent by Mr. Homes for Sarah
to go to the funeral – beg to be excueased, R. And C Lindop called
and said they was going to keep a shop

30th November

Fineshed tharshing the Barley the Old

S&B & S.E.L. made Father 2 new aprons

Fanney went to Mr. Hoboys after a place (see 28.12.40)

1st December

Finished ploughing the Moss Woods – hedging at the Brickel

Went to Tedsley and brot 2 rabbits to back

2nd December

J. Darby paid   6s 0d

Ann Lindop came from the flewbelis, she said we did not want
her, and cryed very much, we said all that words could due but
of now use. Mother slept with her very uncomfortable in the
fur room, she breakfast and the moment after she put on her
things and went to Hatherton, and never said good by to Father
nor Mother (Ann Lindop from Milton? See 28.10.40)

3rd December

Mrs. Salt of Brockton called came to see Miss Heath S.E.L. went
with her to Mrs. G---- for a moment

Uncle Joseph came with Father from wyrley to by an horse of
Mr. Fry and did – W.S. went with to take it home – Father tould
him about Ann Lindop of Milton – it gave great offence that
S.E.L. did not go tow carry Little Smith of the Luce
  (LUCE a nickname given to the Fleur de Lys) (see 28.10.40)

J. Norton bured (Joseph Norton aged just 38) – left 4 small
children and his wife in the family way

4th December

J. Warbank went with Father to Stafford Fair – saw the Fat stock (souls?) bid 27
for an Ox that ws scarce 12 score did not by it

5th December

Paid Thomas Ansloy for Hedging at Wyrley   £1 4s 11d

Paid corbut for turnips   8s 6d

Jack Selvester took pig meat to Wyrley
 Jack Sylvester ag. labourer at Hatherton farm 55 years old.

Mary Askey paid   5s 0d

6th December

Sunday gave poyners cow a norshing drink of gruel and a meat
spoonful of salts – bled her the night before, think her better

7th December

Mother and Sutherns stredend? The flowers

Mr. Prince called and had a game of cards

Grandmother sent some firmity by Thomas

Lord Hatherton's sale – my father and me went and bought
No. 32   £24 15s 0d
 Annual sale of prime fat stock at Teddesley Hall Farm started at
 4.00pm sharp.

And No. 52   £26 5s 0d

And their was a large fat one sold for 41.5.0d.

8th December

Father gone to Rugeley Fair, must have
paid 1s 0d To have seen the show cow

9th December

Father took 3 Lanthors to B. Sollom   2s 10d

And bot beef for Mrs. W.

10th December

Had a poetry book

11th December

They stole a sheep from the late J. G. Stubbs

12th December

Betty Darbey paid   1s 6d

W. Ward fetched coals from Brownhills Old Colliery 2 ton 6   13s 10d

They want Mrs. Hall £47 for house and 11 acres of Land
(at Leacroft) (see 21.9.40)

13th December

Sunday Clark Byrch died
    (Mr. Thomas Birch 45 years Clerk of Cannock Church.
    He resided and carried on good business in the boot and shoe trade
    in a house fronting the Walsall Road).

Mr. Selvester drank tea with us – R.L. gone to Chatcull

14th December

Mother took M.L. to Latherford (see 21/23/10.40)

15th December

Richard and Thomas sent Grandmother a letter for her and she
was very much pleased and he and my aunt went to Walsall on
account of the South Staffordshire Bank

16th December

Father gone to look at the Tedslesey Fat Cow the prize cow/sow

Paid Cheatam on account that the mn that bot it run in, and did
not fetch it, Toft of Penkridge his to give £40 for it   10s 8d

15th December

Got the Barley Rick in at wyrley, the wet got in in places

17th December

Mother very ill – obliged to have Mr. Homes (Doctor)

Kill a cow from Mrs. L. Of Hatherton

18th December

Killed the cow at Mrs. Walhouses – a very nice one in the inside

19th December

Cut it up into a very meny very small pieces

Killed one of the cows that was bot at tedsley

Left J. Warbank to clean the tripe – had but one can of all among them all at Hatherton

Betty Darby paid	1s 6d
Mrs. Price paid	£1 0s 0d

20th December

Sunday Aunt Jane here

21st December

Killed the other cow that came from Tedelesley – both very good ones

22nd December

Cut up the other Teddesley cow – the weight of Mr. Masfin sheep 147lb at 7	£4 5s 9d

23rd December

Mr. Stubbs of the Perhill called was going to see J. Ingram they was all Ill of the small pox – except the Mother

Mr. Ward of Teddesley sent 2 Fessants 2 rabbets and one hair, Uncle Joseph wanted the hair, and had it.

Aunt Jane came again. Mrs. H. Sent Mother some grapes

24th December

Father setled with J. Warbank in Full

T. Goodman (ag. labourer of Hednesford) left unpaid	1s 0d

Mr. Stubbs of Hamerwich called – was going to Bickford to to received his Rent, said aunt Jane must come on Monday (?)

Gave the Man that did Mrs. Knights stone in Norton Churchyard   11s 0d

25th December

Aunt Jane had her breckfast with S.E.L. and Father, Mother had
hers in bed, and then went to Wyrley, was very poorly when her
got their

Faney Barley called and had her dinner with us.

26th December

Southens ? and J. Selvester had their wages,

Father went to Rugeley with the Fat (crossed out?) 4/8 a 6.9
took a rump of Beef and brot 2 zen of candles at 6d1/2d/ per lb –
one oz of Ising glass 14d. Per oz – one lb. Of Tea

27th December

Sunday had a leg of mutton for dinner that R.W.B.Collis gave
Mother it came from one side Liverpool it was 4 lb.
It was beautiful

28th December

Faney Lovet left had a goose from Hatherton
(see 30.11 &19.2.40)

M.L.fetched it – Miss Scarlet called
  (Could she be Doctor's daughter?)

29th December

W. Stibbs from Teddesley called – Mrs. G. & Mrs. L.
From H & E & Ann from Mrs. H

Got the Oates in at the Barn yesterday

30th December

Sold Mr. Tomlinson a cow called Willington   £12 0s 0d

Herd that Mrs. Stubbs was confined the last Monday in the year
(see13.1.41)

31st December

Betty Darby   1s 6d

J. Selvester came

The black cow came from Wyrley the other went

Little Wyrley Hall.

1841

1st January

Association called for Mr. Masfin's sheep

Stole half year – Miss Field (Penelope Field an independent
lady of Cannock aged 65.) had Newspaper 1839

2nd January

R. Lindop went to Wyrley – they had stole 3 ducks from
J. Lindops Grandmother (Mary Walker?)

Gone to see Mr. Meanley (Richard Meanley aged 50 farmer at Norton.)
did not come back till twelve o'clock T.G. (T. Ganderton?)
went with her

3rd January

Charlotte Dean was Ingaged to come on the 5

4th January

Was silein the Middle Sladlands

5th January

Charlotte Dean came

Miss Brassington called

6th January

Paid J. Selvester   6s 0d

7th January

Killed a pig at Wyrley and brought half of it here

8th January

George was very poorly – had Mr. Holmes to him

Miss E. Barlow and Mr. Williams called

9th January

Betty Darbey paid   1s 6d

Miss Hordern settled
    Miss Horden is the School mistress- been there since 1834 and ran a
    girls' academy.

8th January

Father settled with Uncle Joseph in full

3rd January

a thunder storm – it struck 2 Church Steeples

12th January

Mr. Scarlet (Doctor) called instead of Mr. Holmes to see George

Thomas and Richard came from Wyrley and brought some
pig pudding

Mrs. Knight sent some sausage

13th January

Paid 5d for a pain of glass in the back kitchen – 3d.
For painting the bucket

10th January

Snowey Sunday

11th January

Gorde (George) very much better

J. Lindop came from H

Father £25 owes 20

13th January

Father and T.W.L. gone to Wolverhampton

Bought a ¼ of a lb. (8d) weights – a frock for me 4.6d. &
steel 2/ and hat 2.6d. George a cap for Thomas – Sarah a
handkerchief 3.6d. father a slock(?)

Herd on Friday that Mrs. Stubbs baby died suddenly (see 30.12.40)

Broch 4.0d. neckless 6.0d. brim(?) 1.7d Gip cloak 14 making 0.11.0

14th January

Setled with Mr. Bowdler for W. L. Gilpin (his agent or manager)

For coals and Timber and scythe   £1 11s 2d

15th January

Mr. Hubert paid his Bill

Mr. Price paid (Thomas was a scythe plater living in Cannock.)   £1 0s 0d

Father gone to Wyrley with Mr. T, Knight it was 11 o'clock when
they came back night

Mr. Brown brot the money from the hall check   £57 18s 4d

Mrs. Hall Bill   £36 4s 4½d

Ours   £27 3s 0½d

Our Bill from Mrs. W.   £2 4s 4d

16th January

Bot 3 lumps of salt   2s 4d

Paid J. Benton (John Benton, farmer living in Hednesford aged 50.)
for Veal had Dec. 30th   9s 3½d

paid Mr. Marshall Drugest 3s 6d

Betty Darby 1s 6d

An Earlin Lamb (B C i s amed??)

Mr. Homes came back had been out
severl days (see12.1.41)

Shops in Market Square, Cannock.

17th January

Making dress 5.6d. new plad 14.9d.

18th January

Flannel 1.11 4 Hank 3.6. pocket 6 Bonnet 7.4. pet l.4
Collar 6d – h/k? 1/21.6

Stock 1.6.2. to Bx 12.6 Bonnet 1.5.0.Shel 7.10 (yr?)
Book 16.6 NF 14.0

19th January

Gave Jack Selvester   5s 0d

Mr. T. Knight (Probably son to Mrs. Knight but does not live in Cannock.)
called and tasted our wiskey said it was good

20th January

S.E.L. finger bad

Gone to calving Hill for a walk

Mothers Brother called tould us that Mr. Werilow had taken a
good farm

20th January

Old Mrs. Selvester poorley at Mr. Lindops

Mrs. J. Pickrell setled (Wife of John ag. labourer of Cannock)

21th January

Mrs. Holland setled – Mrs. Wood was Over and Mr.

22nd January

Put 51 strike of Oates in the room at the barn with out bags

Trubshaw setled

23rd January

Had Mr. Hawkins machine began at 8 o'clock left of at ½ past 4
was Wheat

24th January

Sunday Uncle James diend here

Mrs. Knight had got a very dredful cold

25th January

Mr. H---- Machine today began at 3'oclock thrashed and
½ hours and then gived over to winnow for 2 hours, had
done by 4 o'clock it was wheat

26th January

Sold R. Lindop 66 strike of Barley at 4.10d. per strike took
it in and took the machine to Wyrley

27th January

Thrashed weat at Wyrley today fetched Mr. Wrights sheep
5 yesterday

28th January

Fineshed thrashing at Wyrley

Paid the Machine for 3¼ at 12/- per day   £1 19s 0d

And 1/-d. For himself

The rent day was at Walsall on the 26 of this month

29th January

Mrs. Knight coals 2ton 8cwt (?) at 8/-d/ per ton   19s 10d

T. W. Lindop went to Wyrley

30th January

Sent J. Lindop 20 strike of Potatoes at 5/-d. Per bag   £2 10s 0d

Maid of Potatoes befor   £7 10s 9d

Ward went befor supinup and did not com till morning

M. A. Lindop came from Mr. Shaws to stop one weak F. Barloy
came with her, banns was very late they stop all night

31st January

Selvester and Ward of a drinking

Betty Darby   1s 6d

Paid J. Selvester   16?

Mr. Wright of Wolverhampton   £5 19s 0d

Paid for 1840

Aunt Jane came to Mrs. J.E.

2nd February

Ward came, went to church Bridge for coal   7s 9d

Sent 30 strike of Barley to make Malt to R. Lindop

W. Stubbs Brot a pig for Mrs. Knight
– Father cut it up sent Gorge Lindop
2.6d. by Father for a cristmas box, a
very snowey day

New Penkridge Road School.

3rd February

Mrs. H. Sent to pork pies

Herd that they broke smiths windows over votein

4th February

Mrs. Byrch from Huntington brot 10.0d. towards the harvest
quarter

Corbot came from Wyrley the wite cow got cold Father went

5th February

Sold Mr. Cotton the weat for 9.4d. per strike

Mr. Brinley brot the new salt coffer yesterday

Uncle Joseph Lindop behaived very shabby over a calf sold it
him then Smith

Paid Miss Marshall for my bonnet and ribbon   2s 5½d

S.E.L. went to see them at Hatherton

Mother went in the Eveing to see Mrs. L – it was dredful cold,
Mrs. L 51 yrs old on that day (Mary Lindop – farm 30 acres)

Mary Askey paid	5s 0d
Aust 10 owed 2.6d. paid at twice	8s 0d

Thomas and Ward whent to Wyrley to whiner the weat but the
wind was do high that they could not, aunt Jane at wyrley

7th February

Thought of stoping Sacrament but did not finally agreed with
E. Barlow (Edward Barlow aged 25 a new labourer to live in.) to come
on the 8th of Febery and he did by 11 o'clock

8th February

M.L. bot one point of Gin at Withnalls (Royal Oak) 20 pence
per point

Mr. Prince called about the rooms at the Barn house

Mr. Masfin setled with Father

W. Marshall (Marshall was a headborough.) called for the fire
office premium 4.0d. was paid, and his paid yearly

9th February

Mr. T. Hall called for Mr. Macdurmott quartily pay (He was the
curate and therefore paid by the community.)
(see 12/13/17. 7.40 &13.5.41)

Ward went to Wyrley Bank took coals from Bakers to Wyrley 1ton 6cwt	3s 7d

Brot 37 bags of wheat back to Mr. Cottons, New wheat and
3 Horses brot it Gipsey, Merriman & Sharper/Sharker?

Richard Simms (was an ag.labourer who worked for Joseph at
Little Wyrley) went to be at Wyrley on the 8th helpt them
winnow the Wheat

Fredk Pratt road a race today a bay horse, six years old, twenty
miles in an hour, won, three minutes under time
(as reported in the *Wolverhampton Chronicle*)

> *"The Friendship of Cannock Chase"* by Pitman, Chapter "Old Sportmen
> with Long Memories page 192.
> "Drury was one of a large company of spectators who saw Frederick
> Pratt, of Saredon Mill, ride, for a wager, a horse named Spectre from the
> Swan Hotel, Wolverhampton to the Greyhound, at Yarlett Hill, Stafford,

Saredon and newspaper cutting of Mr. Pratt's race.

MARCH — Yesterday (Tuesday) a match came off on twenty miles of the road between this town and Stone, finishing at the bottom of Yarlet Hill, four miles beyond Stafford. A brown horse, belonging to M . E. Pratt, of Saredon, was backed by his owner to go the distance in one hour, and Mr. Pratt started at twelve o'clock from the Swan Hotel, in this town. Half the distance was performed in good style in twenty-seven minutes, and the match was won with three minutes to spare, without either horse or rider appearing at all distressed. The match was for 50*l.* a-side, and owing to the severity of the weather, the betting was rather against the horse till the start, when his condition and style of going reassured his backers, who then showed freely at five to four on him.

a distance of twenty miles, well under the hour. For the entire length the road was covered with ice, and at times the going was exceedingly difficult"

Note: William Drury was landlord of The Crown Hotel, Cannock and was also an Overseer of the Local Highways in 1845 and was one of the most respected men in Cannock.

10th February

Sent 43 bags of Wheat old, to Mr. Cottons took it at twice,
Mr. Prince was very insiltin about S.E.L. (see 3.12.40 &8.2.41)

11th February

Setled with Mr. Hall M

Mrs. J. Lindop came about potatoes

Fetched coals for us from Queens Colur   14s 9d

Brot the chatcull cow from Wyrley to kill tomorrow

12th February

Sent potoens J. Lindop   £2 10s 0d

Paid W. Lindop of Hather for one sheep   £1 15s 0d

First sheep Lambed in the rick yard at the Barn

13th February

Betty Darby paid on 6th	1s 6d

Paid Mr. C. Worsey Church levy — 7s 6½d

Mrs. Knight sent Gradmother a bottle of wine port

Charlott Dean went home on the 12 about 4 o'clock with a
pain on the stomach (see 9.6.41)

Sold a deal of the Chatcull cow

14th February

Ward took Mutton to Mrs. Hawkes

Mrs. G. Hawked was confined of a nother daughter on the 5th
(see 9.5.40)

W. Stubbs was Married on the 10 to Miss Kenrick of shifnell
to Sharshill stubbs

15th February

Emma Dean come insted of her sister because Charlot was Ill
(see 13.2.41)

Butler gone to help to thrash at Wyrley

16th February

Paid a man sent by Mr. Hanbury Church Rates –
Arblaster was is name (1833 Walker 10.1/4) — 12s 11½d

Father gone to Wyrley brot the cart tire from Gilpins 1.3.10d.
at 15/-d. Per cwt 1.7.6d. 23.1/2 lb. Nails 3 /-d.(?) per 5.10.1/2
took to Mr. Brinley — £1 3s 10d

17th February

Wards box 16.6d. turnick paid it

T.W. Lindop went to rumer Hill Mr. Halls to skin one sheep
that wanted

18th February

T.W.L. took 2 heifers to Wyrley and some sheep

Suped last night at Mr. Cot? Mr. S. Wright and Mr. Prince
(see 10.2.41)

19th February

Set some turnips in the Gardin for seed

Father went to Wyrley saw Mr. Somerfield saw J. Lindops calf

20th February

Mrs. Collis died this morning at 3 o'clock

Soed the brickel wheat with Mr. Masfin drill, the big pig ridd
in (3 strike of wheat)?

Paid Mr. Poyner   £11 3s 6d

Mr. Holms was robed last night of brandy and other things

Betty Darby paid   1s 6d

Mrs. Dawson said the first weak after Christmas 21 Sunday
the pretty horses past through

22nd February

Father went to Huntington

S.E.L. and G.L. went to Wyrley with Father he bot some rails
and stumps of R. Tufft   14s 6d

Bot 2 cows of J. Lindop and a calf

Had a pair of scissors 2d.

Men had tea kettle mendid 10d? Left 2d. To prove it

5d.? For Humberellor paid the 2 Aust 3l?

23rd February

Cleavland Street Mr. Acutt lives

15 per lb. For suscex hops whole pocket or half paid Mr. Acutt
on account   £5 0s 0d

Father gone to Walsall S.E.L. and J.L. with him, bot a fish,
and for the seat in the Church (Moriness?)

Setled with Withnalls (nusure?) Legs with Mr. Prince their

24th February

Ash Wednesday Father was at home went to settle at the crown
but did not, they tould him about the bad land

NEW PENKRIDGE ROAD, CANNOCK. G.470

25th February

Brot a calf from Uncle Joseph, S.E.L. and G.L. came from wyrley
and aunt Jane came with them went to sleep at Mrs. K
(see 27.2.41)

26th February

Came and helped us with the cushinon in the Church

Paid Mr. G. Gilpin for the cart tire   £1 8s 0d

Setled with Mr. Biddle

27th February

Grandmother very unwell aunt Jane obliged to go home because
she was so poorly (see 25.2.41)

Mrs. Collis (curate's wife) beried

28th February

J. Darby paid   1s 6d

Mr. Hemson preached.

Had Mr. & Mr. S and Mr. J.L.

1st March

Charlot came back and Emma went home

Mr. Hawkes was looking at the large pig in the stye
(lived at Norton Hall.)

Ward began to plough the over field and Huntington it had
been graised for more than three years has not paid for trouble

Setled for all Buxtons? New and sp----?

In Jar 12 Bottles Sherry and one pint

1 Jar of Brandy 27 (oz?) & Gin 27 (oz?)

3rd March

Took R. Lindop 54 Strike of Barley (see 8.3.41)

Brot the Malt back 39 strike sent 30

Paid Mr. T. Lindop	£7 0s 0d
Left unpaid at Wyrley	£20 0s 0d
Paid Mr. Tomlinson in full up to day	£13 10s 0d

4th March

Father went to Millers sale of Otherton bot a covered cart	£6 10s 0d

Paid for painting it	9s 6d

S.G. was their was very much pleased with the new light gates

5th March

Killed Holland cow

6th March

Weghd the large pie 21 score 5 lbs.

Father paid Mr. Jenney? For black cow (see 31.3.41)   £7 0s 0d

Mary Askey paid 5/-d. Owes 16 at 3 of March

Father took the meat to Wyrley stoped at the luce Mr. Hawkes
Byches had the hams of the pig 7 lb. Came (1.18.0?)

4th March

Bot 3 Pigs off Mr. Cotton each paid for them on 23   £1 4s 0d

6th March

G. Lindops new boots of E. Byrch   4s 6d

Bot Mr. Sheridan calf 7¼ lb

7th March

Got 14 Lambs paid R. Sims   £1 12s 0d

8th March

Brewed 5 strike of Malt(20 – 1.7.0) that was maid at R.L (1.17.0)
(see 3.3.41)

Brot the Poney from the Hills

9th March

Lucy left wyrley T Bar & E.L. – cn?

10th March

Beautiful day, ward drawing the Manure out of the field down
Hatherton Lane that Father bot of Mr. Tibbets oweing to
Mr. Foster (see 19.8.40)

11th March

T.W.L. gone to Latherford

Mr. Benton bringing us seed from Rugeley – onion seed 6 ---- 2 oz?

Mrs. B paid 2.6d. for seed sowed 2 oz it

12th March

Paid ----- lower garden Smiths of Wyrley	17s 11d

Saw Mr. Vincet and Miss Hand

Had the chimney swept paid	(1) 3s 6d.?

13th March

Setled with Mr. Fry

Received Wolverhampton and Staffordshire Banking Company check with Gr. Gilpins name on No. 301 dated March 1st 41	£11 19s 0d

Received of Mr. W. L. Gilpin ten£ (see 16.3.41)

Stuckely's Banking company Somersetshire – Bank payable
Messrs Robarts, Curtis, Robarts, Curtis & Co. London No. 1725

14th March

Mother went to see both the babys at Norton Hall and was very
much pleased gave her some cake to give the children
(G.Hawkes Esq. Norton Hall)

S.E.L. drank tea at R.L. first time

Betty Darby paid	1s 6d

15th March

Modus Vicar of Biskbury ?

1.10 ? 8/-d. Or 8d.? For a poors Rate for Essington
Made 1st Sept 1840 sent by Mr. Prince Sims

Garden in at the barn Arblaster

13th March

Mary went to Long with Mrs.

14th March

Went to Longchurch (could be Longdon) and saw Mr. Dawes
father and he was in 37 year his lady and she was blind

15th March

I came back with Mr/s? Arblaster to Parkgate and there I came
back with Mr. Leadbeater to Cannock

Cannock.

Mother bought milk pan and joul for 13(shillings or pence?)

Bot ten sheep of Mr. Twig at 45/-d. A piece   £22 0s 0d

16th March

Settled with Mr. Cope in full

Paid Mr. Hanbury tithe   £7 15s 0d

Setled with Mr. W. Gilpin (see 13.3.41) Mr. Boudler did for
Father had made the bill against himself

Father and Uncle Joseph went to Chatcull paid U stopt for
interest 1.0.0d.   £9 15s 0d

Mr. Fry left Cank (see 13.3.41)

One lamb died wile Father was a way put another one the Ewe,
got 27 lambs

Father bot a cow of Uncle John   £5 10s 0d

And the cheese per hundred it is £20 that   £3 7s 0d

Uncle John owes father out of the £30 that he had at the sale

Paid Grandmother at Chatcull 3.0.0d. for the Money that had like
to bin lost

Cilled a cowe that came from Uncle Joseph

Paid Mr. Smith of the sun for ale
Inn and Taverns
Crown Inn- Thomas Leadbeater
Roebuck- John Smith
Royal Oak- Edward Withnall
White Swan- Daniel Grocott
Beer Houses -
William Belcher
Thomas Sellman- The Black Horse
Samuel Smith- The Sun

Lord Wrottesley died on the 17th March at Wrottesley Hall he
was in his 70th year

Lord Hatherton's Diary – March 23rd We went to Wrottesley's to attend
the funeral in the Monckton's carriage. Much melancholy on the road.
Found at Wrottesley's Lord Dartmouth, Sir. J. Boughey, and several others.
The late and present Lord Wrottesley's were behind a screen close to the
mouth of the vault in the Chancel. Dartmouth, Lord Talbot and I went in
one carriage together, and were 4 of the pall bearers. I could not quite
dry my tears whilst carrying the remains of my departed friend.

Created a Baron in 1838 and was an MP for the city of Lichfield for

18 years (1820-1838). He was a Whig politician and was also a founding member of the Royal Astronomical Society and was a well-known astronomer in the mid 1800's.

Betty Darby paid   1s 6d

George poorley

22nd March

Father fetched the cow from Safford T.W.L. drove her did not pay
for her then bought a wagon cloth   8s 6d

23rd March

Gone to settle with Mr. Cotton in full, received   £112 0s 0d

Paid S. Greensill 1841 £3.0.0d. towards her Intrust –
1844 Apriel 1st paid S. Greensill 3.0.0d. towards her Intrust 1845
paid 2.0.0d. Sept 17th 1847 paid Mrs. Cotton 3.0.0d. for Intrust
(5/-d,)Aug 31

There was a Sarah Greensill aged 25 living at Wryley with her mother
Hannah aged 65 running a farm with brother William aged 20.

Mr. G.J. Stubbs Sale – Mash tub copper 4 quart – brass candlestick
– brass ladle – part of brass dreger 1 3 6 glass brandy bottle 2.6d.

24th March

Bot a cow of J. Benton   £9 5s 0d

J. Barby paid   5s 0d

25th March

Paid Crutchley 1.13.0d.

Received of R. Lindop – gave back 5.0.0d.   £20 0s 0d

Paid G. Strongitharm   £13 0s 0d

G.J. Stubbs sheep   £21 15s 0d

(?) saddle child   2s 6d

26th March

Took Mrs. Selvester of little W – that lives at J. Lindops money
back that was borrowed on the 30 of Octr to pay Mr. Tibbitts
but could not get the (time?) made so did not use it – paid for
Interest 1.17.6d. (see 19.8.40)

27th March

Sowed the peas at Calvenshill had Holms drill paid 2s 6d

Mr. Wood called bot see Barley 5/-d.? Per strike is to have 30 strikes

Aunt Jane called

28th March

Sunday T.W.L. at Wyrley

Early 6/-d.? Per strike before 12.10.9d. – May 62.5.0 ?

29th March

Sold Potatoeas £3 15s 0d

Ground 9 Strikes – April 16 of Malt of Mr. H. Measure £3 7s 6d

30th March

Brewed 9 strike bot 2 lbs. Of Hops of Mr. R. Bailey 3.0d.

Began to pull the Tithe Barn on 29

Father bot the thatch that came off 4 waggon load gave for it and doors 2.0.0d. paid for it on 30 April

31st March

Settled with R.W.B. Collis

Wrote a letter to the C – W – Hoverseyer of Norton that he will not accept the office of Gardion

Sent the cowe that came from Mr. Jenney to Wyrley (see 6.3.41)

1st Apriel

Had some strawberry roofs gave me

Cut the pig up at Wyrley

Brot a (Sparrither?)

2nd April

Killed that pig that bot of T. Warbank had it 35 weeks it was 15 score

1st April

Fetched a cow from T. Wrights price did not pay for it £19 15s 0d
    Thomas Wright was a farmer aged 59 living at Huntington with son
    Samuel aged 30 and daughter Jane aged 14.

3rd April

Mary Askey paid 5 owes 1 6

Bot of Mr. Hadcock Vally $£12 15s 0d

Betty Darby paid 1s 6d

4th April

Mother went to the mill

5th April

Killed one cow of T. Wrights

J. Warbank was here

Grafted a tree for Apples – set some herbs

6th April

Mrs. Knights coals $£1 4s 4d

Washed some sheep in calve in hill pit

J. Warbank been here and at Rugeley

Bot Mother some tea and coffy

7th April

Sowed the soot at calvenshill and rolled the peas

Mrs. Barlow and Mr. Williams and little abram called

8th April

Mother went to Stafford to meet the cheese with Father
(from Chatcull?) brot them had 36 Cheeses – Mr. J. L. Daughter
came with us – Mr. Tomlinson of Stafford brot (M&?) Cousin –
Mother spent 2.7.0d.

9th April

Good Friday price paid 1.0.0d.

Bot a cow of Mr. Somervill $£7 0s 0d

Killed a lamb that was lambed 12 of Febr

Gave Mrs. Hawkes one (Zr?)maid 1.2.6d. on the other

10th April

Had a side of veal of Benton, sowed the Barley in the Sladlands
and the seeds

11th April

Paid R. Sims 15.6d. before 3.9.0d. – April 24 paid Sims 12.3d.

Sunday

12th April

Got ready for the thrash in machine

The fresh schoolmaster called a bout R.L.

13th April

Eliza Lindop (from Hatherton) called – Mother wonted to know
what she had done at her

14th April

Sent R. Lindop Barley 63 strike at 5/-d. Per st

G. L. & R.L. came from Wyrley

15th April

Fetched coal from C-Bridge   5s 0d

Herd that Barber & Marshall had stopt

16th April

Sent potatoes Bloxwich   £2 7s 6d

About the (7?) fetched a calf of Mr. Cotton was to be a soverin bid
not pay for it

17th April

Betty Carby paid   1s 6d

18th April

Brothers brought some May flowers

J. Shorter brot M. Lindop from is home (SEL married James Shorter in 1843.)

19th April

M.L. of C and SEL went to Bloxwich

Ward brot some hay from Wyrley

20th April

Sowed the Barley at Huntington

Had Holms drill paid him 3.0d. at the same time

John Warbank had a cowe from Wyrley

T.W.L. Brot a nother here

Paid M. Marshall for Making M.L. Frock 2.6d. –
Ling? & hook & thread 1.7d.

21st April

Fetched the beef from Rugeley Father did

J.W. paid to the rest

22/23 April

Father went to Stafford to meet some sheep fror Chatcull of
T. Lindop 16 sheep and 5 lambs

Herd that Spilbury broke

23rd April

Father took Beef to Bloxwich – brot SEL and ML to Wyrley
left them

24th April

Mr. Byrch birthday is eather 96 or 97
   Henry Byrch, independent gentleman of Leacroft.

Herd that Sanders had the bailiff

Mr. Walmsly left yesterday

Setled with J. Buxton in full

Had 3 men at Huntington working at that house that Byrch
lives in – 26/-d. Per day for thatcher & 3.10d. for the macon
and 1.0d. for T. Butter

25th April

SEL at Wyrley (see 23.4.41)

26th April

Mrs. Wood came Father gave him young keeper

TWL took the cows, Father bot to Wyrley

Paid Mr. Poyner assessed Taxes £1 2 s 11d

Land Tax 2.0d. Hunt (---)?

Setled in full with R. Witehouse

The Whitehouse's home and blacksmith's forge, Hatherton.

27th April

Sold the cowe that Bot of Benton and that came from Hatherton
in the summer

SEL came from Wyrley (see 23.4.41)

28th April

Fetched coal to hear 3s 8d

Setled the Bill with Haddock £5 3s 0d
(A farmer from Coleshill.)

Killed the last pig at W

Sowed the Barley on the first of May in the Blakefield, it rained after

29th April

The churchyard trees nearly in full leaf, and a tulip quite open

30th April

Father went to penkridge Fair

Paid Mr. W. Harrison for Lime due at Xmas 40/
£3 8s 0d

Sold six beast and bot two

1st May

Mother went with Chatcull Mary to Stafford – brot her new gown

Herd the cuckow

Father paid her 5.9.0d. for a cow her brot her on 22nd March

Mrs. (Messenger?) Died Dropt suddenly of her Chair when it lighted – killed a cow that had of Mr. J. Lindop
    Charles Messenger lived in Great Wyrley and died 1844 aged 77.

Too J.S. nails back

4th May

Mr. R. Bailey (aged 61) Died – sent 12 sheep to the common

Sold Mr. Wood 8 sheep Bot of Milner cows

5th May

Father went to Wolverhampton

Setled with Fisher in full

6th May

Sent J.L. Potatoeas worth 2.5.0d.

Paid J. Lindop when he came to the (asca ont?)   15s 7d

Gave RL one shilling

Killed a calf of S. Wr---- (Wright?)

7th May

Sold Buxton a leg of veal

Bot 2 Lamb of S. Wright   £2 0s 0d

8th May

Weight is calf

Sold Mr. Hadcock of Coleshill 5 sturkes 2 year olds   £38 10s 0d

9th May

Beried Mr. R. Bailey aged 61 years (see 4.5.41)

Selvester of H had is tea with us

10th May

Mary Askey paid 4.0d. owes 18.3d.

Betty Darby	1s 6d

Beried S. Harvey of Huntingdon (Samuel aged 61)

Father taken 2 stirks to ley – one that he bot of Adcock of L.Wy
the other of Milner of Nor Vallue –   (£14 2s 6d/)
  Edward Adcock, a farmer aged 60, and wife Sarah 65.

Ingstry Ley Nomber 32 on the orn?   £14 2s 6d

Grandmother gone with Mrs. Meanley to see her Aunt at Walton
about one and half of ston – was back by half past 5 o'clock –
Mrs. James Stubbs

Took the cow that we have been feeding at the barn

Poyner to Wyrley (WT?)

Brot Boat load of Lime to wedges mills 20 tun W. Jackson steere
(A Jackson family lived at Hatherton (Wedges Mill). Robert
died 11-7-46 aged 64) – **drawed 14 cart load in 8 hours**

Mr. Beck left Somervills (see 26.6.41)

Paid Mr. Hall of R.H. for R.T. Macdurmot (see 12/13/7/41 & 9.2.41)

14th May

Father and Grandmother been at Stafford & SEL enquired the
price of them cakes they are 5.6d. per box, bath something

Father bot some Lambs of (Y?) Mr. Masfin

15th May

G-M went to Wyrley

16th May

Mother and SEL went to church

17th May

Mrs. G. & TG (Mrs. Ganderton and son?) and JW (Jane Walker?)
& SEL went to Teddesley – Father took part of the way

18th May

TW went to Wyrley Father brot a calf fro Uncle Joseph –
Mother and him had words

19th May

Paid Wilkiston Road Bo-ad Leves	16s 11¼d
Paid for Stones 5.0d. in Money	11s 11¼d
Paid Mrs. S. Wright 32.9d.	
Mr. Wright paid T. Wright rent	£3 0s 0d

20th May

Mr. Wood setled with Father

Uncle JW called tried the colt with the oxharrow at the brickel
was very quiet

W. Brown died of Bangley?

21st May

Had one lamb from Wrights the first since settled
(her Majesty's Birthday)

Finished setting the Potatoeas at calving Hill

Mr. Wood washed his sheep at Calving Hill pit – he has taken
the blackfords of Mr. Leadbeater for is sheep

22nd May

Paid Mr. Biddle for painting the cart	9s 6d

Settled with Mr. Sanat on the 20 day

Betty Darby paid	1s 6d

23rd May

Sunday T. Selman gave us a cucumber –
> Thomas Selman kept a beerhouse in Mill Street, known as the
> Black Horse.

Spirit of Armonia Best thing to clean Black without any trouble

24th May

Set the hen at the barn with 14 eggs and at

Mrs. Knight Brot us some apples

25th May

SEL and Ann at Mr. Knight and Father took them and called at
Wyrley took Aunt Jane with them

Setled with Mr. Jesson? For 2 years

SEL bespoke a bonnet (see 1.6.41)

26th May

S. Hedwards and his Father shered 55 sheep–

Possibly Samuel aged 29 who lived in Mill Street. He was a maltster.
His wife was Anne aged 29.

27th May

Mr. Carlet died when he was undress him –

That could account for the two ladies living at the Mill by the time of the
census which was in June.

Put up 63 fleeces

Put the sheep in the common peace weat

Bot of Mr. Wood 10 lambs

28th May

Sent Mrs. Poyner 2 soverin

Spread the Lime at the moss-woods and did it very bad (see 13.5.41)

Had R. Smims all weak

29th May

Jack Darby   4s 0d

Mr. & Mrs. Somerfield called going to Chatcull (see 31.5.41)

30th May

Sunday Fetched the cow from Wyrley that we called poyner

31st May

Mr. Somerfield come back from Chatcull (see 29.5.41)

Mrs. R. Lindop owes more than 60lb for Intrust for £180

Mr. Som bot a cheese and paid for it

1st June

Had Beef

SEL bonnet came (see 25.5.4)

Took J.L. Potatoes – 9 bags at 5/-d. Per B

2nd June

Washed 3 Blankets

Father went to Rugeley

Tok J. Warbank 6 chairs that he bot at N. Brookes Sale received
7.6d. each for them the same that he gave

3rd June

Maid of Potatoes 24.10.0d. besides what Butler? Had

T.L. of H took the colt that he bot of Father to R to try to set
and a black one did not set them

4th June

T. W. & L fetched one Lamb from T. Wrights of Huntington

5th June

Sherring sheep

Herd that Mrs. Barlow house was part Burnt

The Cottage, Chatcull. A family called Barlow lived here in the 1840's.

Sowed a few turnips for the first time have not been so late for a
many years

Betty Darby   1s 6d

6th June

Mother & SEL and Father stopt Sacrament the Lord have
(mured/nuned?)

7th June

A Sambrook & Father and TWL went to Rugeley fetch
Mr. Woods drill–
    Charles Sambrook was a warehouseman aged 30 living in Mill Street.

8th June

Soed the turnips at the Mosswoods with the drill

Coal church B   4s 8d

½ of Salt and half ¼ of Brandy

9th June

Mrs. Powell stoped all day

C. Dean left (see 13,2.41 & 27.6.41)

10th June

Fetched 5 sheep from Teddesley

2 of Iron Rust mixed in treacle and maid in two pills for Girls

11th June

Sowed the turnips at wyrley

Mrs. Walhouse was not at Church she was unwell

12th June

Father was late at Wyrley

13th June

Sunday

14th June

R. Lindop called with Mr. Holms R had been at penkridge

15th June

Father paid S. Hedwards after shering the Teddesley sheep   10s 0d

16th June

Father went to Wolverhampton

17th June

Norton Club G gone to Wyrley

18th June

Grandmother came

19th June

Betty Darby   1s 6d

20th June

Buttler brot us some new Potatoes the first

Father gone to Wyrley Bank to take tea Mr. S – very Poorley indeed
(see27.6.41)

21st June

Father gone to Walsall

Mr. Horn came to weigh the wool

22nd June

Did today, SEL and TL gone for a ride to Wyrley

Mr. Wright of Wolverhampton called today

Soed some of the brickell turnips

23rd June

Had Mrs. Butler to wash (see 20.6.41)–
   Probably the wife of Thomas Butler, ag. labourer aged 30 living in Cannock.

Grandmother gone to Teddlesy

24th June

Ann's Brother John ill (see 29.6.41 & 2.7.41)

Paid Mr. Goodwin for Church rate   11¼d

Mr Selvester of H here

25th June

GL come from Wyrley

Ward fetched a load of Marl

26th June

TWL took Mr. Shorter some Lamb and two Cheese

Mr. Bic stood corting T. Price in the churchyard
(see 13.5 &12/16.7.41) –
> James Bick is a 20 year old farmer living at Rumer Hill. Single.
> Uncle Joseph questions his sexuality 16-7-41

27th June

Ann Webb came about the place and was to come on the
Wednesday, after and was to have £2.5.0d. at Christmas
and if good 5.0d. more (see 9 & 30.6.41) –
> Ann Webb is the new servant to live in. C.Dean had left.

J. L. Called had seen Mr. Sevester of Hatherton thought
him very ill (see 26.7.41)

29th June

TWL took Ann Hodson (companion of Mrs. Knight) to the
stone hous her Brother died ¼ beg 10'oclock
(See 24 & 27.6.41)

30th June

Ward fetched coal from Baker   8s 10d

Ann Webb came (see 27.6.41)

~Father came from Wolverhampton

Majority for Scott 23 the Liberal (can?)
Report from *The Staffordshire Advertiser* - June 30th 1941:
The Election at Walsall- Scott and Gladstone- Majority Scott 23 the Liberal
Result - Robert Scott 334
       - Gladstone 311
    The Poll terminated at 4 o'clock in the afternoon 17th June. The
Polling had been nearly at par most of the day, but at 2 o'clock Mr. Scott
was 15 ahead which was increased to 23.
    At the conclusion a vast assemblage of men, women and children
congregated in the High Street. Mr. Scott appeared in the window of
the committee room at the Dragon Inn and addressed the multitude. In
conclusion he exhorted the people not to detract from their victory by any
breach of the peace and he hoped they would use forbearance towards
his opponents.
    During Mr. Gladstone's speech considerable uproar and tumult
followed lasting some time and throughout the speech and he was
interrupted frequently for several minutes at a time.
    J.N. Gladstone was the brother to W.E Gladstone the future Prime
Minister.

1st July

The Club, Father went in to the club room and took a glass or two of wine with the Gentlemen and they charged him 9/-d. – a warning for the Future always take diferant to the rest when you go to a room full of company, Mr. T. Hall of rimer Hill was with him.

2nd July

Killed a calf of Mr. J. Lindop a large sheep and 2 more

J. Hodson beried (see 29.6.41)

Received 2 pair of Gloves

3rd July

Mrs. Wood sent some peas and cherrys for Mrs. Knight

J. Walk called saw G.Mother at (Ted?) from the cows went up selvesters weat at wyrley water barn – very rude indeed about them

4th July

J. Shorter diend here today and John Mrs. S came for tea and went to church (James Shorter SEL future husband)

Jones was beried, he was well and died in a Moment

5th July

Mr. J. Lindop Chatcull paid for cheese   £28 9s 6d

And sheep paid for Intrust 15/-d.

6th July

Hednesford Races

Father went to wyrley the cows had ben hout

7th July

TWL fetched Grandmother from teddlesey

Aunt Stubbs had been very good and comfertiable with her (see 1.9.41)

8th July

C. Dean brot a pair of wood piggens

Mowed part of the seeds at the barn

9th July

Fineshed the Other and them at Calvinghill

10th July

Richard had 3 penney worth of Strawberrys

Miss H gone from home aunt Jane at C at Mrs. (K/H?)

Betty Darby   1s 6d

11th July

Su brot some panseys very wet

12th July

The rent day Benton inside ted Mr. Bick about being at Smiths
(see26.6.41)

Paid Mr. Hall for Mr. Macdurmot lent him an (unn-er?)   2s 6d

13th July

Mr. Macdurmott paid is Bill (see 9.2.41)

Mother drank tea at Mrs. Knights

14th July

J. Lindop called and was very troublesome and offending –
slept in the child bed but did not see us in the morning

15th July

Showery

16th July

Father went to wyrley saw as B. Joseph tould him that beck was
no man (see 13.5.&26.6.41)

17th July

Set Green the house at 1.6d. per weak

Mary Ann Lindop came up from Hath

J. Darby paid   1s 6d

18th July

Mr. Somervill came and went to church and spent the day with us

19th July

Mr. T. Knight went with Father to wyrley – was back by dinner, carried the Sladland clover – should have carried Calving hill if Edw clues had not stopt with is wife

Betty Darby paid   3s 0d

20th July

Rained EC came at night (Edward Clues?)

21st July

TWL Brot the calves from wyrley put them at the barn give them a little hay tea

22nd July

Bot salt 1.6d.

Mrs. Knights coals   £1 0s 7d

Mr. Bysot & Mr. L. Called and bot a leg of mutton

Diend at the Crown had been to look at a race horse the drank one bottle of wine here

23rd July

Carried the clover at calv on the waggins all night top the rick at the barn

24th July

TWL brot 10 strike of Malt from RL

1½ for Mrs. Knight

Fanney Harvy married

25th July

Sunday the Children went on the common

SHOAL HILL

26th July

Mr. Selvester worse (see 27.6.&10.10.41) carried clover from the
Hills 9 Load all there excep 3 children

27th July

Killed a beautiful cow that we fed and bred – gone to carry
more clover

28th July

Father took the wake Beef

Selvesters Farm to be sold did not sel it (see above)

Lent Mr. Buxton 3 soverins

29th July

Mowed the meddows at the brickel – very showery

ESW Ward, T. Butter was in ded by ten – did not begin before
8 o'clock

30th July

One foot thick

31st July

Betty Darby   1s 6d

1st August

Norton wake Mr. Shaw and Mrs. Barlow came over – Mother
went to see Mr. Selvester he was up and better (see 20.9.41)

2nd August

Mr. W. Simkin called

GL new shoes of Mrs. Barns   2s 6d

3rd August

Mother went to see Grandmot fond he pretty much better

4th August

Father went to wolverh

Took the Beef to the Hall saw Selvester(Hatherton?)

5th August

Womans club

6th August

Beried Mrs. Jenney –

Elizabeth Jenney aged 70 wife of James a farmer at Norton.

7th August

Brot the Lambs of Mr. Poyner

8th August

Sunday

9th August

Father had the tooth ake

11th August

SEL went to Mr. Woods to go to Wolverhampton

12th August

Went to the races

We fineshed the hay carrier both the brickell meddowes

13th August

Very wet Sally cooke beried

EL came back from Mr. Woods (see 11.8.41)

Brot the children all toys

11th August

Ward fetched coals C Bridge   8s 4d

S.lea of Cannock Died the same wead as Lady Chetwine –
he was 99 years

14th August

Betty Darby   1s 6d

15th August

Mother and Father diend at Mr. Somerfield and SELindop saw
GL at Mr. J. Lindops – was at home at 8 o'clock

16th August

Washed – S. Grinsell was very unwell

Mr. & Mrs Chaberlin came to the door

Father sold Mr. Cotton weat at 11.6d. per bag

17th August

The weat dropt 6 per strike

18th August

Thrashed weat to day and the (next?) 8?

E. Birch Mutton 2 ½ 1.5 ½ d

19th August

Gave Ann 6/-d. For her Mother

Ellen James brot some Goosberies

Mrs. Wood and Miss Dutton came

Parimacket cloth 4/-d. Per yard

20th August

A chicken leg broke and two lost but due not know were

Sent Mr. Cotton 52 bags of seat at and 10 of Barley –
weighed 10scors 17

21st August

Thrashing the peas

22nd August

Sunday Hatherton wake

23rd August

Mowed Hill peace Sladland Barley

Mrs. L. Of H sent the childr? Some pind---?

24th August

Mother bot a tap of the best metal at the door for   3s 0d

Sold some sheep at the fair

25th August

Cut the peas at carvinshill

26th August

Began to reap at the Moss woods began on the 23 at wyrley

SEL and ML spent the day with Miss Tomas and Miss Wight
of Birmingham

27th August

Tithes for Bloxwich   £1 17s 0d

28th August

Finished riping the Gins weat

29th August

Father took Miss H. Of Cannock and Miss Tomas of London
and Miss H of B to Norton Church (see 1.9.41)

30th August

Carried the Barley at the Sladlands

SEL and ML drank tea at Mrs. H

31st August

Cut the little cow up that we bot of Mr. Somfield in the winter
weighed (Uncle)?

1st September

Miss Thomas and Miss H of Can and Miss H of B went to
Teddlsley with Mother and Tom – drove them in the Trap,
we all drank tea at Aunt Stubbs and say the Hall (Teddesley?)
(see 7.7.41)

2nd September

Carried the wheat at Gins Gap – exclenant horder

3rd September

Rained very much

4th September

Father went to Stafford bot Veal for walhouse – rained all day –
dredful

5th September

Sunday wet

6th September

Finished the Moss wood weat riping

7th September

Miss Thomas and Miss A Knight called at 11 o'clock to --------?
Goodbye were to start in a Chaise at 2 (see 1.9.41)

Coaches from the Crown Inn -
The Red Rover to London at 3pm and to Manchester at 3.30pm
The Aurora to London at 3.30pm and to Liverpool at 10.00pm
The Railway to London at 8.00pm and to Manchester at 11.00pm

8th September

Betty Darby paid – very wet   4s 0d

9th September

Very wet

10th September

Fine turned the Barly at Huntling

11th September

Carried the (?) over field were the Olive bushes grow – fore load

R. Lindop's wife in labour ML going to Wyrley

12th September

R. Lindop's Daughter born at 4.0'clock in the afternoon

13th September

Began to crried the Moss Woods weat brot 2 load by 4.o'clock
fineshed at. The load of peas from calvinghill 2 load of peas
from the Hills – 12 load in all very large loads.

14th September

Very dredful lightning and thunder very wet all day – struck a
cottage at Bridgford, enterd the bedroom shivered one of the
bed posts – a child in bed at the same time escaped –

> The Staffordshire Advertiser -
> During the violence of the thunderstorm on Tuesday night the lightning
> struck a cottage at Bridgeford near this town occupied by a labourer
> named Fletcher. The electric fluid entered the bedroom, shivered one
> of the bedposts, disturbed the bed clothes and passing in a horizontal
> direction to the other side of the room escaped through a fracture made
> in the wall.
>   Fletcher had gone to work before the storm had gained its height
> and his wife had providentially left that part of the bed on which the
> lightning fell. The poor woman, however, who was thought was not
> injured has ever since been very ill through the alarm occasioned and
> has since been under the care of Mr.Perrin, surgeon of this town. She is
> in a fair way of recovery. A child who was in the bed at the time escaped
> unhurt.

The Lord is a God of Knowledge And by Him all actions are
weighed – on uncle Stubbs grave stone hammerwich

13th September

Mr. Masfin carried from 2 in the (morning) clock to 11 at night
60 acrs

14th September

Father bot 1.0d. worth of beesums 12 for the money

The parsons looking at Mr. Poyners farm (Rev. Collis)

15th September

Still wet brewed 3 of S malt

16th September

Finished reping the brickell weat and made a rick of wheat out of
hashforlong

17th September

Carried the blake field Barley 11 large load

18th September

Carried the calving hill wheat and the brickhill – finished and 4 more neighbours

19th September

Went to see R. Lindops first born Mary Ann Barlow Lindop

20th September

Herd poor selvester could not live long (see 10.10.41)

Brewed fair – bot cow

21st September

Ward gone for coals shallow 17

Pheineas Fowke Hussey Esq. Called going to take tea with Mrs. Walhouse again at (3/8?) o'clock for Father to show were Mr. Sant lives he went in the room to him he told Mr. Sant he had had 15 dogs and lost them all thought he should have no more he is as going from hear to join Africa is rigment which was going their he left Mr. Hawke's on the 23 the day that Mr. R.L.

Bottled the Rum 7 large Bottles and 7 Small pint Bottles al but about a tea cup full

23rd September

Instant married the Hon. Edward Richard Littleton the only son of the Rt. Hon. Lord Hatherton, in St. Mary's church Bryanstone Square, London, the Lady Margaret Percy youngest daughter of the Earl and Countess of Beverly.

Lord Hatherton's Diary – There were present – the Beverleys, Wharncliffe, Mrs. Percy, Mortimer Drummond, the Bishop of Carlisle (who officiated) and on our side ourselves, Cynthy, the Cavans, Lady Wellesley, the Duke of Wellington. After the ceremony we all went to a formal sitting breakfast at Lord Beverley's – At 2 o'clock, Edward and his bride went to Oaklands, which the Egertons had lent them for their honeymoon.

At Cannock between 50 & 60 of the principal inhabitants sat down to dinner, and my father was one

Cannock Square.

24th September

R. J. Shield died at Oswestry

25th September

Mr. Sant very unwell

26th September

Ann Hodson very poorley (see 29.6.41) –

Mrs. Knight's female servant.

27th September

Killed the brewed cow

28th September

SEL and Father went Walsall Fair–

By 1839 Walsall had two fairs annually. Buyers and sellers would go from all over the West Midlands.

29th September

Mr. Holland brot a brace of Partridge

30th September

Hd them for dinner

Father gone to Rugeley brot 13.6 of grocery

2nd October

Richard shoes of Mr. Smith paid him   5s 9d

Gorge Lindop had a new pair from Stafford- did not pay for them

Brot 2 new grates for parlour at Wolverhampton for the house at
the barn – had them put down and white washed, and put ready
for to received rent by October 25th

3rd October

Had two fowls for dinner

4th October

Fetched the two heifers from Ingstry paid   £3 5s 0d

Brot the cow from Mr. Salts he would not give him anny thing for luck

5th October

Tueasday

6th October

Mother went to Wolverhampton bot severhall

8th October

T. Lindop had a hunderstanding with R A bout the settling T.L.
owes for Malt and making (?) 36.1.1 R owes for Barley and
meat 46.18.0 – R. Lindop owes T. Lindop 10.17.0 Charges 3 per
strike more than (Nera?) Books?Brooks

DIARY GOES OUT OF DATE AT THIS POINT

22nd October

Coals deep   7s 9d

27th October

Mr./Mrs? Birch of Leacroft died – Buried Nov 4th Age 96

20th November

Betty Darby   7s 0d

10th October

Mr. Selvester died at Hatherton at half past one
(see 26.7 &20.9.41)

| Norton Church gatherd | £7 8s 6d |

24th November

| Mother went to Wolverhampton and Miss Thomas and she bought a warming pan for Mrs. T.L. | 7s 0d |

| Sugar nippers for1 | 1s 6d |

| Bought for a friend ½ Dozen good size Goblets | 5s 0d |

| A Mustard pot lid | 6d |

| New Mustard pot | 1s 6d |

8th December

4 0'clock Wednesday Evening Mr. Brookes took Harriot Barlow down as his Wife was married yesterday as we supposed – they were in a Double Gig another Lady and Gentlemen behind followd down by Mrs. Shorter and Edward Poyner

Mr. Brookes- could be Isaac Brookes (25). Harriot Barlow - Ann's sister?

11th December

| A New pair of shoes | 5s 6d |

15th December

William and Jack went to Mr. Poyners coal pits for a load of coal and ditto sleck William also went to BrownHills for a load – the three load cost £1.0.0d. all but 4d

Year?

22nd January

Settled with Mr. Buxton Miss Field for the newspapers

1842

18th February

Bottled the Brandy and had 14 pint bottles and five large ones full

Bottled the Gin 10 large bottles and five small ones

15th February

| Brewed 9 other Malt from Mr. Hobdys 7.9d. | £3 9s 0d |

8 lb Hops to the Brewing the best off Mr. (Shorter?)

8th March

At Hardwick Chester the beloved wife the residence of her Father John Cottingham Esq. – Mary of Rev. W. Jendwine M.A. late of Sheriff hales Shropshire (see 19.1.40)

10th March

Racked the 9 Strike of Ale put 4 lb sugar and hops

9th March

Mrs. Birch of Leacroft Died Aged 85 –

Eleanor Birch, wife of Henry at Leacroft.

12th March

Sold Mr. Wood 10 bags of Barley at 4.0d. per Strike

Barns street Ridge Wolverhampton

9th May

Mr. Lane of Sutton Bot a cow	£13 0s 0d
Owe Mr. Cartwright	1s 9d
And	2s 0d
Markland -------? R. Curson Gardener 3 Greams for	3s 6d

Where the water place stands was called Tube Hill 5 hundred years ago where Mrs. Benton and (Wilson?) lives was called the old Hall built in Queen Elizabeth's reign and that is her Court of Arms in the Window

The Old Smithy once stood at the top of Wolverhampton Road, Cannock. It was bought well over 100 years ago by a Mr. George Turner , who converted it into a blacksmith's shop. The Old Smithy at that time contained a great amount of panelled oak, and it was reputed that Queen Elizabeth once stayed there. The property was once the subject of arbitration. Negotiations for its purchase broke down at £900, and arbitration resulted in a figure of £1600 being reached.The property then became known to many as 'Tupenny Corner' because it was stated that it cost a twopenny rate eventually. In those days a large amount of shoeing was done there for the horsemen visiting the Crown Public House and the coaching trade. The smithy was eventually knocked down, after standing empty for a long while. In it was an Elizabethan window which bore the inscription 'Honi soit qui mal y pense' (Evil to him that evil thinks). *Cannock Advertiser Centenary Issue 1878-1978* – June 15 1878.

A corner of old Cannock.

9th May continued

1oz of Nutmeg 1/-d. 1 oz of Isinglass 1/-d/ from Mrs. Turners
6 April

29th March

Brewed 3 Strike of Malt 2 ½ worst Hops and one best–
Sent to Wyrley 7 Strike same time

11th April

Brewed 9 Strike of Malt 5lbs of worst hops and five pounds best

12th April

Father and Uncle Somerfield went to Chatcull paid Grandmother
for Interest 3 Sovereigns

Mrs. Bradstock The bridge Crediton Devonshire

19th April

Setled with Benton and paid the assessed Taxes   £1 2s 11d

Land Tax 2.0d. Hunt (?) 7?

Daniel Johnson Hook Gate (near?) Market Drayton

Finished Harvest on the 6th September 1842 – the calvinghill weat

27th July

Mr. T. Lindop of Chatcull came and Father was at the Hills
making hay went to see Mr. Shorter he is very ill –
came and slept here

28th July

Paid for cheese	£21 16s 0d
Came to 22.16.9 ½ d left for Intrust	£1 0s 9½d

August

Came to Mr. Shorters Funeral who died July 39 aged 50 years
(see 12.7.43) –
William aged 50 buried on 4-8-42.

9 of May 1840 Miss Hawkes born

3rd August

Mrs. G. Hawkes (of Norton Hall) died was confined of a daughter
at one 0'clock and died at 7 in the morning aged 36

8th October

Paid Mr. Tompson	£1 2s 11d
Land Tax	0s 7d
(?) Land Tax	2s 0d

21st April

Paid Mr. Tompson comp 1.2.11 Land Tax 2.7d. –
William Thompson, an independent gentleman of Cannock aged 60.

11th October

Brewed 4 Strike of Malt with 3 lbs and half of the best hops

7th December

Brewed 9 Strike of Malt new and 9 lbs of the best hops new &
racked it on 18th put in bag 4 lb of loaf sugar a little parched weat

1843

7th March

Brewed 9 Strike of malt and 9 lb of hops

19th April

Brewed 4 Strike

25th May

Bewed 3 Strike

Mrs. Shorter Married (see 4.8.42)

12th July

Brewed 8 Strike

23rd March

The last Friday in March and the last Friday in September.
The May Catchers always come

17th March

Mrs. Walhouse died buried March 24th 2843 aged 76

5th April

Paid Mr. Tolson for seeds   £4 2s 7d

29th April

Bt (Dudly?) 12 lb Clover seed   7s 0d

Paid June 22

O rejoice Oh rejoice for the Major is come, He is come from the
crown and the Court, Oh rejoice O rejoice for the Major is come,
he is come to encourage our sport

The well wishers of the House of Loynton intend to celebrate the
coming of age of Sambrook H. Burne Esq. By dining R V H in
Newport on wends. 13th Sept Sir T.F.F.Boughey Bart in the chair
Tickets 15/d. Each

3rd October

Went to Chatcull T. Lindop & James Shorter gave Grandmother
£3 for Intruct – bought a cheese back 34 lb. At 6d. Did not pay
for it, and each a couple of ducks

Lector of Vitiorl tak a few drops of water when the cough is bad

Black wool 3.9d. wosted 4.3d.

1844

30th January

Brewed 9 Strike of malt 4 lb when B and 4 lb on 17 of Feb
when stopt up & ½ oz of Gelentine did not rack it

T.L. unwell

Grandmother age 88- Chatcull

1846

10th May

Sent by Uncle Somerfield for one years interest   £3 0s 0d

For my Grandmother at Chatcull

1847

5th November

My Father and George went – Interest   £3 0s 0d

1850

5th March

Interest – Mr. Sayer (Menteritting?) Father

1851

20th May

Paid Interest – Mr. Sayer went again

1843

2/3 ? November

The Most Honourable Henry William Marquess of Anglesea
came to the Court at the crown inn Cannock -
   Probably to elect the town's officers.

Rubub & Colunna an (eaqu?) quart as much as much as will lie
on one shilling for palpitation of heart – R.F.T. Blackburn told us

Salomonia drops for the tooth ach – Sweet Spirit of Vitre two teaspoonful

For a scald Head recently discovered Pyraginus of Acidetous Acid – it is the
strongest white vinegar distilled from the other vinegar –
just tuch the places with it

1845

22nd February

Bured Mr. Samuel Barlow at Broughton aged 58 years – on
18th ult at the house of his son-in-law Mr. Richard Lindop
Tittensor, Mr. Samuel Barlow, Chatcull aged 58 years, highly
respected by all who knew him

At Cannock on the 22nd instant aged 49, Mr. Michael H. Walker –
Commercial traveller, for twenty six years the able and faithful
representative of Messrs. Gilpin, of Wedges Mills, edge tol
manufacturers – April 1848 (see 28.6.40)

1845

14th July

T. Butler Mowed the Brickel Meadows – Carried them on
Friday July 18th

1845

31st March

Sir

I beg leave to state that Mr. Thomas Lindop has been suffering from severe illness, and is now labouring under a Disease of the Heart which renders him an unfit Person to serve on a Jury as the excitement thereby occasioned might hurry the circulation and produce a recurrence of the attack.

I remain

Your Obdt Servt

Thos Holmes – Surgeon

Mr. Wm Smith – Bailiff of the Hundred of Cuttlestone

1846

1st February

Mrs. Knights birthday Aged 82

On Tuesday last Sept 1 at Norton Canes, on the body of Richard Simms, a labourer aged 22 who met with his death under the following circumstances. On the Sunday Evening before the deceased with three companions had been drinking at a public house in Norton until about ten 0'clock when being turned out by the landlord they went to Mr. Kendricks barn to sleep there. In the barn was a cart load of barley which by some means or other not shewn in evidence was tilted up and which falling upon the deceased suffocated him before he could be drawn out. Verdict – died from suffocation

2nd April

Sent James Shorter 3 Bags of Peas and 3 bags of Barley (SEL married James Shorter 5.7.1843) – Sent 30 strike of Barley to Mr. Boulders and had make 37 Strike of Malt out of the 30

1851

T. Greensill June 13 was 22 years old

141

Cannock Sept 23/46

Dear Sir

Mr. Lindop whoo tells me that he purposes seeing you tomorrow had requested me to write to you respecting that part of Calvings Hill land that was last purchased by Mr. Barber. I can only say what must have been apparent to yourself when you looked over it that it is weak land and in the worst possible condition and requires that great indulgence should be given to a good Tenant which I am sure Lindop is to enable him to bring it about. I hope yhou will come to a satisfactory arrangement with him which will be mutually advantageous to both of you. Tomlinson who looked over the barn with myself has not yet began the necessary repairs but I expect he will soon do so. I am yours truly

W. B. Collis (Rev)

Mr. Wathew – Iron Founder – Westbromich

1847

13th April

Borrowed of Mr./Mrs? Shorter six ham bags

5 drops of sweet Nitre in ½ a tea cupful of chilled water for a child when it is hot and feaverish – as many as 30 drops in a day

Also Mary Relict of the above? Who died April 20th 1849(7)? Aged 73 years both of Little Wyrley (Could by Mary Lindop)

Blessed are the dead who die in the Lord

1852

3rd July

My Grandmoth at Chatcull died in her 91st year of her age and was intered at Eccleshall on the 8th July

Trinity Church, Eccleshall

12th December

My Beloved Mother Died and was interred at Cannock on the
17th of December Aged 47

Cannock Feby 2nd 1850

Sir

I beg to inform you that I recd your favour of yesterday. I cannot
conveniently obtain a post office order here, or I would forward
you the amt of Tithe due from me to the Vicar of Walsall.
I will take the earliest opportunity of paying it to you at your office

Remarkable plant Victoria – Aust 8th 1851 (M.Lake?) Regia saw it

1850

February	
Church Rate Cannock	£4 6s 0d
(?) Huntington	17s 7½d
Paid George Tomlinson	

1847

Bought of Mr. Thos Bedward a large shaw? Knife Engine	5s 50d
Of Mr. Withnel Turnip Engine	£3 3s 0d

1848

New Brass Cap to the Gig wheel from Mr. Bedd paid

1850

Of Proctor & Byland/Ryland? New plough paid	£5 7s 3d

Written sideways = a little water White soap (Rottentone)
Hartshorn boil it up

1846

8th May

Received from Mr. Richard Meanley Ten Pounds for half a years
Rent Due Lady day last for a Moiety or Equal half part of the

Norton Common and Newlands estates, and 5/-d/ towards a
Dole to the Parish of Norton Due 2lst of Dec last. William Stubbs
Excutor to the Estate of the late Thos Walker

From 1840 – 1847 several pages of accounts (no names) which are
included in the original transcript

Pantichnethaca Clothing establishment S. Hylam Proprietor,
23 New Street, Birmingham August 7 1857(or 1851) –
Mr. S. & T.L. went

For Rumatism one penny of Hartshorn spirit 1(oz?) of camfor
pounded 1(oz?) sper of Tirpintine – quinine, or salt of bark (dear?)
Ipecocuaha or vomiting root

1842

27th August

Paid Mr. Timmis of Rugeley for Vetches   17s 0d

Extra Phenomenon: Derby. On Thursday week, during a heavy
thunderstorm, the rain poured down in torrents mixed with half
melted ice, which battered against the windows in large patches, but
incredible as it may appear, hundreds of small fishes, and frogs in
great abundance descended with the torrents of rain, the fish were
from half an inch to two inches long, and a few considerably larger.
We have heard of one weighing three ounce, some of the fish have
very hard pointed spikes on their back, and are commonly called
sticklebacks. Many were picked up alive. The frogs were from the
size of a horse bean: numbers of them came down alive and jumped
away as fast as they could, but the bulk were killed by the fall on
the hard pavements. We have seen some alive today which appear
to enjoy themselves in a glass with water and leaves in it. Derby
Reporter – *Staffordshire Advertiser* July 17 1841

The first ingredient in conversation is truth the next good sense the
third good humour and the fourth wit.

Why must we honour and obey our parents – Because the eye that
mocketh at his father, and despiseth to obey his Mother, the ravens
of the valley shall pick it out, and the young Eagles shall eat it –
Prov 30 17 verse

Blessed are the peacemakers, for the shall be called the children
of God – Matt 5 V93

Who hateth his Brother is a murderer lst John 3

Woman comes forth as a flower in the field and is soon cut down

Oh come, then, to our fairy bower: Our holiest time is the moonlight hour, and never was moonlight so sweet as this

Since God is ever present ever felt in the void waste as in the City full and were he vital spreads there must by joy

Unto the upright there ariseth light in darkness. The righteous shall not be afraid of evil tidings, his heart is fired, trusting in the Lord

Where we thing or feel most, there we always speak least

The Lord is a God of Knowledge: And by him are all actions weighed

The eagle's force subdues each bird that flies – What metal can resist the flaming fire – Doth not the sum dazzle the clearest eyes – and melt the ice and make the snow retire – The hardest stones are pierced through with tools, The wisest are, with princes, made but fools - Written by Henry 8th and sung to Anne Boleyn during their courtship (Henry 8th was renowned for his love of music, writing poetry and songs)

1847

Mrs. Knight died on the 28th January Aged 83. On the 16th March Father walked with Mr. Thos Knight J. His son (Monkton?) to Birmingham to take a wagon load of goods, and came back about half past ten 0'clock on the same night

20th April

My Dear Mother died 74 year of her age one of the best of Mothers

1850

21st October

Received Interest – Decr 9 1852   £1 0s 0d

1851

1st November

R. Lindop left his Father & Mothers home at half past 5 0'clock
with onlhy good morning

1850

21st October

On front cover of diary - Remove not the ancient Landmark,
which thy Fathers have set, Unjust is he and unbeloved of God,
Who scoffs whatever his fathers did decree. He may remove their
landmark from the sod, but nought more prosperous will ever be
– no more: Where ignorance is bliss, tis folly to be wise – Grays
exclamations

1851

1st November

The rose which glares upon the day is never so much sought as
the bud enwrapt in the foliage

Dare to be true, nothing can need a lie – a fault that needs it most
grows – thereby. So much for falsehood which is the principle and
fountain of all sin

I don't like the peach that falls from the tree I like to see it ripen

It should be white as milk Quintum Bark, Medicine

It is only when the mind is at ease, that the body is delicate

1 PART OF THE LINDOP FAMILY TREE

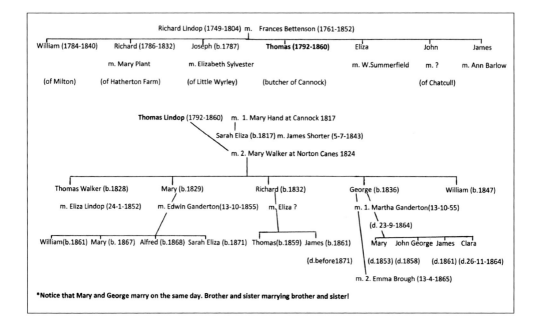

*Notice that Mary and George marry on the same day. Brother and sister marrying brother and sister!

2 THOMAS LINDOP'S WILLS

With regards to his youngest son, William.

As Trustees of the will Thomas Blakeman, miller of Cannock, and James Gardener, gentleman of Rugeley, agreed to look after William's maintenance and education until he reached 21 years old.

He left William three properties. They were as follows:-

1. A cottage with outbuildings, yards, gardens and appurtenances in Cannock (No. 433 in the Tithe, namely the shop, etc.) The tenants later were Thomas Cadman, Thomas Onions, Robert Hand, Abraham Trubshaw and finally John Wright.

2. The land in the Parish of Cannock known as Middle Cow Pasture.

3. Another piece of land at Middle Cow Pasture.

NOTE: As he had already moved to Wolverhampton where he was a grocer, living at 26 Canal Street on February 2nd, 1868 William sold the two parcels of land (2 and 3) to Thomas Rock, blacksmith of Cannock, for £27-0-0.

With regards to the remainder of his children.

I give all my real and personal estate to James Gardener of Rugeley, gentleman, and Edward Smith, machine maker of Great Wyrley, to sell by public auction or private transaction and convert the monies arising from such sales to pay the following:-

1. All my debts, funeral and testimony expenses.

2. One fourth of the remainder to be invested in stocks, funds or securities of the United Kingdom and pay interest and annual proceeds from those to Eliza, wife of my son, Thomas Walker Lindop, and their children after their deaths. If any of those children dies unmarried before they are twenty one years old then their monies are to be split between the remaining sons or daughters.

3. As for the remaining three fourths of the trust monies they are for my children, George Lindop, Richard Lindop and Mary Ganderton (Diary author) to be equally divided among them.

4. I have not made any provision for my son, William, and I declare that my reason for not doing so does not arise from any want of affection for him, but from the belief that he has already been sufficiently provided for by me.

The will was witnessed by Thomas Kennedy and Edwin Joseph Foulk.

3 INDEX OF PEOPLE

Acutt 100
Addams 68
Alsop 27, 44
Anslow – thatcher 7, 18, 37, 39, 75, 87
Arthur – horse trainers 8, 58, 62
Arblaster 99, 105
Askey (Mrs) 6, 37, 56, 61, 85, 87, 97, 103, 109, 113

Bailey 20, 21, 26, 42, 108, 113
Baker 97, 121
Balam – labourer 71
Bamford 41, 51, 57
Barber 13, 110 ,142
Barley 66, 90
Barlow – castrator 6, 11, 34, 69, 92, 97, 109, 118 134, 140
Barns 125
Batty 80
Baxter 13
Baynbarn 33
Beaman 9, 85
Bedward 143
Benton – farmers 20, 57, 93, 103, 107, 110, 112, 123, 135, 136
Beverley 131
Bick 20, 114, 121, 123
Biddle – painter/glazier/tailor 9, 16, 18, 35, 36, 42, 101, 116
Birch 15, 16, 20, 25, 63, 68, 77, 80 and many more
Blackburne – curate 22, 139
Booth 21
Boughey – baronet 106, 138
Boulton 58
Bowdler 93, 105, 141
Bradford (Lord) 74
Bradstock (Mrs) 136
Brassey 12

Brassington (Miss) 91
Bright 56
Brindley - wheelwright 31, 43, 72, 74, 75, 96, 99
Brookes - farmer/malster 9, 10, 20, 24, 30, 37, 38, 42 and many more
Brown - independent 25, 47, 93, 115
Burne (Esq) 138
Bussell 56
Butler - washerwoman 47, 99, 118, 120, 140
Butter 111
Buttery 6, 29
Buxton 50, 79, 82, 102, 111, 113, 134
Byrch - independent 8, 103, 111
Bysot - gentleman 124

Cappell 28
Carr - horse trainers 23
Cartwright-gentleman 135
Cavan 131
Chackett 20, 54
Chamberlain 24, 62, 71, 127
Chetwine (Lady) 126
Clavering 13
Cliff - servant 46
Clowlow 56
Clues 124
Collins, Christina 12, 47, 48
Collis - Reverend 16, 19, 22, 23, 30, 54, 55, 57 and many more
Cooke 20, 126
Cooper (Mrs) - farmer 53, 59
Cope - draper 16, 39, 42, 57, 82, 105
Corbot 96
Corn - butcher 20, 35, 36, 47, 48 ,52, 76
Cotton - mill owner 7, 24, 29, 30, 40, 41, 52, 61 and many more
Cottingham 135
Crosser/Croper? 65
Crutchley 107
Curson - gardener 135
Curtis 69, 83

Darby - blacksmith/tenant 6, 25, 28, 30, 33, 34, 36, 42 and many more
Dartmouth 106
Davison - surveyor 11, 24, 25
Davis 50

Daw	35, 74, 78, 105
Dawson	29, 43, 100
Dean – servant girl	6, 91, 99, 119, 122
Drummond	131
Drury	97, 98
Dutton (Miss)	127
Edwards – sheep shearer	117, 119
Egerton	131
Emmery	39
Fargisson – labourers	66
Farrington & Sons	10
Field – physician	20, 91, 134
Fisher	113
Fletcher	130
Flintoff – horse trainer	79
Forrester – farmer	7, 41, 43, 65
Foster	103
Fowke Hussey – gentleman	15, 131
Fry – surgeon	11, 25, 86, 104, 106
Ganderton – bakers	9, 18
Gilpin – coal & iron masters	7, 16, 19, 33, 45, 51, 53, 54 and many more
Gladstone – candidate for Parliament	121
Goodman – labourer	61, 89
Goodrich	8
Goodwin – gentleman	46, 83, 84, 120
Gough	50
Green (Mrs)	74, 123
Greensill – farmer	44, 107, 127, 141
Grey	15
Gripton	36
Haddock	109, 112, 113
Hall – farmer or shoemaker	9, 24, 25, 43, 44, 46, 55, 69 and many more
Hanbury – independent	16, 23, 99, 105
Hand (Mrs)	13, 56, 104
Harrison – coal owner	59, 112
Harvey (Mrs)	114, 124
Harvison	70
Hart (Mrs)	84
Hatherton, Lord – nobility	7, 12, 13, 21, 87, 131

Hawkes – Reverend and wife	11, 16, 19, 54, 64, 75, 99, 102 and many more
Hawkins – farmer	6, 94
Heath (Miss)	43, 86
Hemmingsley	8
Hemson – preacher	101
Henny	79
Hill	8, 20 ,45, 55, 56 73, 77
Hobbey	79
Hoboys (Mr)	86, 134
Hodson – servant	16, 37, 121, 122, 132
Holland – apprentice surgeon	26, 72, 94, 103, 132
Holmes – surgeon	6, 19 ,44, 65, 86, 89, 92, 93 and many more
Horden – female schoolteacher	23, 92
Horn – wool worker	120
Hubert	28,93
Hylan	144
Ingram – labourer	89
Jackson – grinder	6, 114
James	65, 127
Jendwine – vicar	26, 53, 60, 135
Jening – road surveyor	23, 77
Jemey	68
Jenny (Mrs) – farmers	24, 56, 57, 69, 79, 103, 108, 126
Jervis – Swinfen	14
Jesson (Esq)	30, 50, 116
Johnson	136
Jones	122
Kenidy – schoolteacher	82
Kenrick	99, 141
Knight – independent	7, 16, 18, 23, 30, 37, 40, 42 and many more
Lander	8
Lane (Mr)	135
Lea	57, 126
Leadbeater – farmer	63, 105, 115
Lewice – priest	80, 84
Littleton (Hon)	131
Lockley – bricklayer	6, 18, 36, 40, 46
Lovet – servant	6, 35, 64, 72, 90

Macdurmott – curate/tenant	64, 97, 114, 123
Mann	58
Marshalls – apothacary/dressmaker	9, 18, 30, 37, 53, 54, 93, 96, 97, 110, 111
Masfen – farmer	6, 13, 16, 20, 22, 38, 40 , 46 and many more
Massey – Cross Keys owner	8
Meanley (Mr) – farmer	91, 114, 143
Measure	108
Messenger (Mrs)	113
Miller	10, 84, 102
Milner	113, 114
Morgan	8
Morris	8
Moseley	34
Norton	87
Oakley	38
Oldham	14
Palmer	23
Paget – (Marquis of Anglesey)	12, 139
Parker	15
Parkes	84
Peel, Robert	8
Percy	131
Perrens – tenant	24, 30, 31, 43, 130
Pickrell – farmer	94
Powell (Mrs)	119
Poyner – farmer	7, 16, 25, 26, 28, 43, 44, 55, and many more
Pratt – farmer at Saredon	11, 97
Prince – watchmaker	46, 55, 98, 99, 100, 105
Price – painter/glazier	6, 26, 32, 40, 47, 53, 59, 62 and many more
Roberson	24, 47
Rochell	20
Rogers – cooper	54, 60, 71
Rye	13
Salt – gentleman	86, 133
Sambrook – warehouse man	119
Sanders – farmers	45, 111
Sant – gentleman	16, 20, 30, 36, 44, 54, 80, 116, 131, 132
Savage	13

Sayer	139
Scarlett – doctor	61, 66, 90, 92, 117
Scott – Liberal candidate	121
Selman – publican	116
Selvester – farmer	11, 23, 24, 28, 44, 46, 62, 65 and many more
Shaw	32
Shenton	54
Sheriden	13, 30, 41, 103
Shield/Shiel – parish curate	21, 44, 132
Shimel	84
Shorter – grocer/draper	21, 40, 61, 67, 110, 121, 122, 134 and many more
Shute – tradesman	36, 51
Simkin (Mr)	125
Simms – labourer	11, 97, 103, 110, 117, 141
Smith, J. (Norton farmer)	21, 38, 67, 82
Smith, J. – Shoemaker	24, 38, 56, 67, 76, 77, 133
Smith, J. – Roebuck	106
Smith, ?. – Fleur de Lys	86
Smith, W. – Coal master	23, 30
Sollom	88
Somerfield – uncle to Mary L.	15, 34, 42, 68, 100, 117, 126, 128, 136, 139
Somervill – surgeon	8, 33, 68, 109, 123
Southern – labourer	11, 23, 30, 39, 71, 84, 85, 87, 90
Spilbury	111
Stanley – Lord	12, 81
Stokes – farmer	126
Stringer – shoemaker	20
Strongitharm	59, 107
Strutt	76
Stubbs – independent	8, 16, 31, 45, 46, 51, 53, 54, 58 and many more
Talbot, Lord	106
Thacker	65
Thackery – farmer	82
Thomas	20, 69, 128, 129, 134
Thurston	54
Tibbets	70, 82, 103, 107
Timmis	144
Tolson	138
Tomlinson – builder	16, 33, 39, 40, 44, 46, 58, 66 and many more
Tompson – govt. official	137
Trubshaw	20, 94
Tuft	29, 88, 100

Turner	70, 135, 136
Twig	105
Urpe/Earp – engineer	20
Vincent	104
Wade – gamekeeper	39, 63, 74
Wakelin	14
Wallbank/Warbank – labourer/butcher	6, 30, 34, 47, 50, 55, 64, 65 and many more
Walhouse – Ld. Hatherton's mother	7, 13, 21, 25, 38 54, 56, 64 and many more
Walker J. – family relative	21, 24, 44, 50, 54, 56, 57, 62 and many more
Walker M. – Gilpin's rep.	55, 61, 140
Wall	9
Walmsley	25, 111
Ward – farmer/labourer	6, 23, 30, 45, 47, 50, 76, 85 and many more
Warilow	94
Wathew – ironfounder	142
Webb	6, 51, 57, 65, 79, 121
Wellesley, Lady	131
Wellington	131
Wharncliffe	131
Whitehead – labourer	61
Whitehouse	28, 112
Wilkes	8
Wilkiston – govt. official	115
Williams	63, 69, 82, 92, 109
Wite/White?	128
Withnall – publican, Royal Oak	61, 82, 97, 100, 143
Wood	6, 25, 26, 43, 54, 56, 63, 74 and many more
Woodward	78
Worsey – butcher	55, 99
Wright	13, 23, 24, 28, 33, 39, 42, 43 and many more
Wrottesley, Lord	106

BIBLIOGRAPHY

Cannock Advertiser 1890's.

Cannock Census 1841.

Chatcull Census 1841.

Diary of Mary Lindop aged 12.

Graveyard plan of Holy Trinity Church, Eccleshall.

Hednesford's Horse Racing History – Anthony Hunt and John Griffiths.

Lord Hatherton's Diary.

St. Luke's Births, Deaths and Marriage Records (1820-1870).

Staffordshire Advertiser (1839–1841)

The Cannock Chase Coalfield and its Coal Mines –

Cannock Chase Mining Historical Society

The Friendship of Cannock Chase – Pitman

The Lindop Family Tree by Nancy and Geoffrey Lindop.

Tithe Map of Cannock 1841.

Tithe Map of Chatcull 1846.

Various Lindop family wills and land agreements.

White's Directory of Staffordshire 1834.

Wolverhampton Chronicle 1840-41.